Researching Practice in Ministry and Mission

Formission Ltd
Rowheath Pavilion
Heath Road
Bournville
Birmingham B30 1HH

Researching Practice in Ministry and Mission

A Companion

Helen Cameron and Catherine Duce

scm press

© Helen Cameron and Catherine Duce 2013

Published in 2013 by SCM Press
Editorial office
3rd Floor Invicta House
108–114 Golden Lane,
London EC1Y OTG

SCM Press is an imprint of Hymns Ancient and
Modern Ltd (a registered charity)
13A Hellesdon Park Road
Norwich NR6 5DR, UK

www.scmpress.co.uk

British Library Cataloguing in Publication data

A catalogue record for this book is available
from the British Library

978-0-334-04624-0

Typeset by Manila Typesetting Company
Printed and bound by
Ashford Colour Press Ltd

Contents

Acknowledgements

We would like to acknowledge Sue Rodd, John Caperon and Tracy Robinson, whose unpublished research has been used as case studies. We thank Andrea Kelly for her observations on the needs of practitioner researchers. We thank Brian Marshall for an earlier version of the six-point plan. Thank you to Mark Read for the diagrams and to Phil Coull for the indexes.

Three readers who represented the different readerships of the books commented on the manuscript most helpfully. OxCEPT kindly funded a transcript of our intensive research methods course. A final word of appreciation to all those who have attended research methods courses either of us have taught. Your questions have helped us write this book more than you can imagine.

List of Illustrations

Introduction

If you want to research practice in ministry and mission, you are engaging with the field of practical theology. Practical theology enables those engaged in ministry and mission to think theologically about what they do and to draw belief and action closer together. As a rapidly developing sub-discipline within theology, practical theology is attracting growing numbers of students from across the Christian tradition. This book welcomes that flourishing and seeks to accompany those setting out on the journey of researching practice.

This Introduction contains essential material if you are to make sense of this book. It sets out the purposes of the book and who it has been written for. It introduces the authors who will act as companions talking you through the process of designing, conducting and writing up your research project. It then invites you to examine your motives for undertaking research before reassuring you that you already have many of the skills that good research requires. The final part introduces two important theological issues: What is practice? and How does practice relate to theology? Like the chapters in the book, this Introduction finishes with some questions that you may find helpful to address before moving on to the next chapter.

This book can be used at a number of stages in the research process. If you are thinking of undertaking a course of study that involves research, it should help you get a sense of what will be involved. If you are about to start a research project, it is designed to give you a step-by-step plan for managing your project so you can schedule it around the other realities in your life. You may be a more activist learner and so have already started your research and got stuck. This book tries to identify some of the more common problems researchers encounter and suggest ways round them. However, a successfully completed research project is like building a house: if the foundations are dodgy, it is unlikely that the completed house will stand up. This is reflected in the book's structure, as it is Chapter 7 before we get round to conducting the research.

The purpose of the book and its audience

There is no shortage of books on how to undertake research. However, this book is for a particular audience and brings three purposes together. It is written for people engaged in ministry and mission, who wish to research either their practice or aspects of the Church and world that provide the context for their practice.

The three purposes of the book are to demonstrate:

1 how to design research that enables questions about practice to be answered
2 how to understand the underlying approach or methodology of research
3 how to manage a piece of research as a project alongside other responsibilities.

Most research methods books focus on one of our three purposes, but we want to bring them together as being of equal significance in successfully completing a research project.

Few books on research methods are aimed at those working in theology. This one affirms and seeks to build upon earlier books that emphasize the importance of methodology for practical theologians. To take two key examples:

- Elaine Graham, Heather Walton and Frances Ward in their book *Theological Reflection: Methods* offer a vision of the practice of theology as 'a disciplined reflection, providing indicative models of understanding [of] how talk about God emerges from human experience and questions' (2005, p. 8). They identify three practical tasks for theology, namely the formation of character, the building and maintaining of the community of faith and the communication of faith to the world – all tasks with which the researching practitioner can identify.
- John Swinton and Harriet Mowat in *Practical Theology and Qualitative Research* look at the normative role of theology as revealed truth. They advocate 'critical faithfulness':

> Such a form of faithfulness acknowledges the divine given-ness of scripture and the genuine working of the Holy Spirit in the interpretation of what is given, while at the same time taking seriously the interpretative dimensions of the process of understanding revelation and ensuring the faithful practices of individuals and communities. (2006, p. 93)

This book arises directly out of our experience both as colleagues undertaking research together and also as teachers of an intensive course on research methods. Both these experiences convinced us that there was room for a book that avoided the 'cook book' approach – follow these instructions and you will produce something as ideal as this picture. Our approach is to engage with the messy reality of research and talk you through some of the common problems researchers face, particularly in faith-based settings. We also wanted to write the book because we are convinced that thoughtful research can enable ministry and mission to achieve greater faithfulness.

The purposes of the book now need spelling out in more detail.

How to design research that enables questions about practice to be answered

It sounds obvious, but research needs to be designed in such a way that it produces the answers to the questions you want to ask. This means understanding different research methods and what they are likely to produce. The even-numbered chapters give you an introduction to the five most commonly used research methods in practical theology, highlighting the particular issues that arise in a faith-based context and giving examples of how we have used them. These chapters also look at the limitations of each method. Learning to design research is a craft that involves learning from the experience of other researchers and getting feedback on the design you intend to use.

How to understand the underlying approach or methodology of research

There are different approaches to doing research, which carry different assumptions and therefore affect the way you design your research. Doing research in theology, which is particularly interested in beliefs and assumptions, means it is important you understand the approach you are taking. Methodology is the term used for 'approaches to research'. Different research methods can be adapted to make them suitable for particular approaches.

How to manage a piece of research as a project alongside other responsibilities

Many books on research methods assume that the researcher is working full-time on their research with few distractions. For most people studying ministry and mission the opposite needs to be assumed. They will usually be doing their research part-time alongside a demanding work role and domestic

responsibilities.[1] Each part of the research process makes different demands and planning for these demands can ensure a finished project. There are two types of research project – perfect
ones and finished ones. Our aim in this book is to show how
you can avoid catastrophic mistakes, learn from the minor mistakes that will inevitably be there, but above all, have a plan
to finish.

Finally in this section, we want to say more about the people
for whom the book is intended.

Masters and doctoral students in practical theology, missiology and ministry

If you plan to do research that takes you beyond a library or
archive into the world of practice, then this book will give you
a framework. If you are on a Masters or doctoral programme,
there should be much in that programme that reinforces and
supplements what this book offers. If you are doing a part-time
PhD or an MPhil, there may be much less support and so you
will need to work harder at putting the structures in place that
you will need.

Supervisors of research projects

The rapid growth of practical theology means that a good proportion of those supervising student research projects will have
had no hands-on experience of conducting research on practice
themselves. It is hoped that this book will act as a pedagogical
aid to such supervisors. The key points at which students get
stuck are identified and activities suggested to help move things
on. Often the most helpful thing you can do is take the student

---

1 Full-time students have more opportunity to mix with professional
researchers and ask questions in passing.

away from the task that is defeating them and suggest something else which may enable them to see the task differently. We have taught supervisors and students together, and after an initial reticence they have found it helpful to swap perspectives on the research process. Talking to your student about what you agree and disagree with in this book can help diffuse the false expertise that students sometimes expect of supervisors. Having a more experienced colleague to turn to is important if you are to give your student the feedback they need to complete their research and pass their degree. For doctoral students, annual reviews of progress are vital to ensure that the project is on track and that you are meeting the expectations of both the university and student.

Sabbatical and practitioner researchers

For many people, it is working towards a qualification that provides the necessary spur to learn how to research but there is no reason why it shouldn't be a regular part of being a reflective practitioner in ministry and mission. It is tempting to feel that practitioner-initiated research doesn't need to follow the rigours of work done for a degree, but giving in to that temptation often means a piece of research that isn't completed or fails to have the impact the researcher desired. It is a good idea to find someone who will supervise your research, ideally with a Masters or doctorate in a relevant discipline. The hope is that this book will act as a companion in working together. Appendix A highlights some particular factors to bear in mind.

Leaders in ministry and mission

Leaders are often expected to make use of the results of research to shape policy or practice. This book should give you sufficient insights into the way in which research is designed to evaluate the quality of the research you are being asked to use. It can be tempting to use the phrase 'research says . . .' to make your point. However, the claims made for research are often exaggerated and in faith-based contexts, and research which is illuminating in one context may be misleading in another.

Like all worlds, the world of research has its own jargon. Because the book is written for a number of audiences the following terms are used to simplify the text:

- Researcher – anyone undertaking a piece of research.
- Student – someone undertaking research specifically to gain a degree.
- Dissertation – the writing up of research for academic purposes – for Masters students it is usually called a dissertation and for doctoral students a thesis.
- Supervisor – the person advising the researcher on their project and guiding them as to the standard required.
- Mentor – a person offering support to the researcher as they manage the interaction of their research with their other responsibilities.
- Ministry – work done by anyone whether lay or ordained, paid or unpaid, full-time or part-time which they regard as part of God's mission to the world.

Introducing the companions

In this book we share something of our experience and development as researchers. We also talk you through the process of doing research from our perspectives. So unusually for a book on research methods we want to share some information about us, to help you evaluate what we say. As we have already said, practical theology is a rapidly developing field and so you will come across approaches that differ from ours and as you grow in experience you will want to challenge what we say. Practical theology encourages reflexivity, that is the ability to acknowledge how your experiences shape your assumptions and so your research.

Helen Cameron

My interest in researching practice developed during my doctoral studies. I retrained as a social scientist (after a first degree in theology) by doing a Masters in Social Policy at Brunel University and received some excellent teaching in methodology and methods from Dr Johnston Birchall (now a professor at Stirling University). This was before the huge burgeoning of books on research methods and before much training was given to doctoral students. I had the benefit of studying full-time for my Masters and some periods of full-time study during my doctorate. It was only when I started to teach part-time Masters students in practical theology that I realized how important it was to bring together the project-management elements of doing research with the methodology and methods.

After my doctorate I was fortunate to get lots of experience designing research projects to answer questions being asked by the organizations commissioning the research.[2] This focused me on getting a good match between the questions being asked and the methods used even when this involved persuading those commissioning the research to be more adventurous than they initially wanted to be. During this period I co-edited *Studying Local Churches* (Cameron, Richter et al. 2005), which tried to show the assumptions that four different disciplines brought to studying the practice of the local church. I also developed a personal assumption that you only really learn what people believe when you see what they actually do.

Being an academic involves supervising students' research, acting as an examiner of dissertations and theses and reviewing articles for academic journals. All this develops skill in evaluating the research of others and learning lessons for your own practice as a researcher. My own early education was somewhat variegated, and so I've always been interested in how people learn. This book is a reflection on some of the common problems people experience in undertaking research and how they can be overcome.

---

2 These were mostly denominations and faith-based organizations.

From 2007 to 2010, I set up the Oxford Centre for Ecclesiology and Practical Theology (OxCEPT) at Ripon College Cuddesdon. This research centre brings the research approach of practical theology to bear on issues in ministry and mission. An important collaboration for OxCEPT was with the Pastoral Studies Department of Heythrop College on the ARCS project (Action Research: Church and Society). As a research team we realized that we were trying to develop a more collaborative way of doing research that started with the agenda of the practitioners rather than of the academics (Cameron et al. 2010). OxCEPT also provided the opportunity for Catherine and me to collaborate on an intensive research methods course, which was open to Masters and doctoral students and their supervisors as well as sabbatical researchers. Teaching this course convinced us of the value of giving people an overview of the whole process.

As a practical theologian I took a step closer to practice at the end of 2010, when I became Head of Public Affairs for The Salvation Army. Lobbying policy-makers and politicians means having the data to back up your assertions, and so this role is full of conversations about what constitutes credible data and the practical challenges of assembling it without getting in the way of the 'real work'. The role also offers challenges about how to do theology in the public square so that it is integral to what we say about what we do. Moving on from OxCEPT generated a 'legacy moment' making me want to pass on my enthusiasm for well-designed research in the service of ministry and mission.

Catherine Duce

My interest in this book stems from ten years' experience of researching practice in church-based settings as a student, researcher and practitioner exploring my vocation in ministry.

I first trained as a social scientist, studying geography as an undergraduate at Newcastle (2000–04). At that time I took for granted the expectation that as part of the preparatory work for completion of a final-year dissertation I attend a year-long training module in developing research skills. The encouragement of my supervisor, Professor Nina Laurie, who had extensive experience of fieldwork overseas, led me to spend the summer of 2004 in Ecuador interviewing Ecuadorians about their experience of living in separated households caused by migration of family members to Spain. Faith emerged as a significant coping mechanism for these people, whose stories were rarely told or heard. These early interview conversations instilled within me the conviction that data gathered in research could equip people to explore their own questions about practice and life circumstances.

With the help of a research scholarship I remained in Newcastle to complete a full-time Masters in the ESRC-recognized research training programme. This Masters is commonly regarded as a stepping stone to doctoral studies in the social sciences. It focused upon many of the skills introduced in this book. In some senses it was theoretical and idealistic (given my recent experience of the messiness of real-world research), but I can now appreciate that this course provided a methodological foundation rarely afforded to newly registered professional doctoral students in practical theology. It certainly helped me complete a Masters in Pastoral Theology at Heythrop College (2008–11).

My plan to complete a doctorate was interrupted by two consecutive research jobs. First, at Durham University in Community and Youth Work (2005–7) mapping out faith-based youth work across the North East (Ahmed et al. 2007). Second, as fieldworker of the ARCS project (2008–12) (See *Talking about God in Practice: Theological Action Research and Practical Theology*, Cameron et al. 2010.)

These jobs have given me first-hand experience of the challenges of conducting faith-based research – at times the loneliness of it, the constant bridging of different disciplines, the sensitivity and patience required to communicate between academic and practitioner worlds, the working alongside overstretched practitioners coping with the unpredictability and busyness of daily life in ministry and mission. I have been grateful over the years for supportive friendships developed at termly London BIAPT (British and Irish Association of Practical Theology) group meetings and at annual BIAPT conferences.

Yet the joys of this work have far outweighed the challenges. They have compelled me towards practice. As pastoral assistant at St Martin-in-the-Fields (2011–12) I experienced first-hand the tremendous potential of bringing research and reflective practice skills into the field of ministry. Now in full-time theological education, I carry with me a fascination for practice which I hope will sustain me in future.

This is the third book we have designed together. We feel there is a balance to be struck between being logical and linear and providing a structure that triggers learning. The book has two types of chapter. The odd-numbered chapters (authored by Helen) describe the process of designing, executing and writing up a piece of research. The even-numbered chapters (authored by Catherine) each introduce a particular research method and discuss its pros and cons with some real examples. We could have grouped these together but our experience in teaching suggests that it is helpful to get to grips with research 'as a practice' at the same time as you learn about the process. There is a constant danger of becoming idealistic about the perfect piece of research you are going to produce. Reading about reality as you progress helps keep that danger in check. Once you have designed your research you will want to loop back and reread the parts that refer to the methods you intend to use. It is perfectly possible to dip into this book using the contents and index but we hold on to the hope that you will want to read it all!

We are taking a conversational tone in this book to emphasize that doing research is a practice that involves lots of different conversations. We will also say bluntly some things that supervisors sometimes struggle to say to researchers. For example, 'this project is too large' or 'you do need to finish your literature review before you can finalize the design of your research'. Like all of us, supervisors sometimes put off the difficult conversation, so we hope this book will encourage you to seek feedback at the crucial points in the process. Another part of the conversational approach is the use of metaphors and illustrations. We've tried to use the ones which former students have said stick in their minds as a useful summary of part of the process. At times we've had anxieties about whether we have been too honest. Will people think they can learn anything from two research practitioners who have made so many mistakes? We've tried to balance it with things we think have worked well, but again our aim is to dethrone any ideal research project you may be tempted to put on a pedestal.

At the end of the odd-numbered chapters we have summarized the content by providing a list of questions to reflect upon at this stage of the process. Good design is all about good decisions, and the aim is to highlight the decisions that will most influence the progress of your research project.

Why do research?

Martyn Percy, the Principal of Ripon College Cuddesdon, uses a shorthand phrase to describe the purpose of ministerial training in the Church of England, namely, to produce curious curates. The aim is not to produce people who feel fully equipped for their first ministerial role as a curate but rather people who have a sense of wonder at the work they are called to do and questions they want to ask about how it can be done faithfully. Initial training for ministry aims to give students a firm grasp of the Christian tradition through the study of the Bible, doctrine and church history. It also seeks to give people a framework for understanding their ministry by learning skills of theological reflection and pastoral practice. However, if curiosity is not awakened, the real learning cannot take place when that initial preparation engages with the context in which the curacy takes place. Sadly for some, growing experience in ministry and mission can lead to a loss of curiosity about what is going on. Research is a proven way of reawakening that curiosity and from it a desire to discern what the missional task is in any particular ministry context. Zoë Bennett expresses it like this:

> God has made human beings to be curious creatures. The desire to learn, to find out where someone else is coming from and why others think and act as they do, is a wonderful antidote to judgementalism and narrow-mindedness. Curiosity is a driving force in learning; it may also be a driving force in loving. (2004, p. 28)

Postgraduate study has become much more available to those in ministry over the last 20 years. In some church contexts a postgraduate qualification has become a marker of potential for positions of greater responsibility. There is a possibility that some people will undertake research mainly for the credentials it will secure. This motivation can leave you poorly prepared for the personal challenges that undertaking research pose. For example, in certain ministerial roles people become more accustomed to giving feedback rather than receiving it, and so it can be testing to find that there are non-negotiable standards upon which your supervisor will rightly insist.

There are advantages and disadvantages in using a postgraduate degree as a framework for learning to research. The advantages are that you will be given a structure within which to learn and a peer group to encourage and support you. You will also be expected to work to deadlines, and for some of us these are vital to triggering action. The downside is that there are more and more rules and regulations to fulfil in postgraduate study, and although these have been designed with the students' learning in mind, it can often feel that they are designed to safeguard the university. It can sometimes be difficult to separate the 'real learning' which is relevant for your ministry from the 'academic hoops' which are necessary to obtaining the qualification.

If you are contemplating a doctorate there are additional factors that need to be thoroughly worked through. A doctorate is a sizeable commitment. Typically for a part-time student it will last five or six years. You will have to stop doing some things you enjoy during that time to make space for the doctorate. You will need to negotiate the time you need away from your family and your work. You may need to renegotiate this time as your understanding of what you need to do changes during the course of the research. Your relationship with your supervisor will be central to your success, and so you need ideally to choose someone with a track record of successful and timely completions and ensure that there are structures in the university to which you can refer any problems in the relationship. Changing supervisor is not impossible, but it is damaging to your and your supervisor's reputation, and so it is better to engage actively with difficulties in the relationship as they occur. Helen asks potential supervisees what they envisage the doctorate will lead to. This is to check from the outset that this is a project they envisage completing. A doctorate should be a springboard to a new phase of ministry. There is a danger it can turn into a shed, that is, a place of retreat from life's demands and where there is no clear expectation of what, if anything, might be produced and when. Chapter 3 contains advice on not turning your research into your life's work. There are now a number of helpful books on the questions to ask yourself before committing to a doctorate, of which Phillips and Pugh (2010) is the classic and Smith (2008) helpful for professional doctorates. Read one of these books, reflect and talk to those who will be affected by your decision to do a doctorate.

The transferable skills you bring to research

Having issued some warnings about understanding your motivation, this section aims to encourage you that you probably already possess most of the skills you need to be a successful researcher. The main challenge is to become aware of how you practise skills you take for granted such as reading and writing so that you can adapt them for this purpose. Here is a summary of the skills.

Observation

Ministerial practitioners often have good 'people watching' skills. They are used to noting changes in behaviour and demeanour and seeking explanations for them. They are often practised at watching people interact and seeing what develops from those interactions. In research, the additional skills you need are planning what you will observe and how you will record what you observe for later analysis.

Reading

Reading is such an everyday skill that we have mostly lost any conscious understanding of our habits and practices as a reader. Reading for the purposes of research means being highly selective in what you read, reading it for a purpose and having a reliable method of retaining what you read for future use. For those contemplating a doctorate we would recommend a speed-reading course – not because speed is the issue but because it sharpens your skills as an effective reader.

Listening

Again this is an everyday skill in pastoral ministry and most practitioners have built up skills and techniques that they find effective. For research there is a need to revisit these skills and find out which will enable you to draw out the information you need from people.

Writing

The thought of writing a lengthy report or dissertation can put people off research. Writing for research involves breaking the task down into manageable parts. Most supervisors insist that you start to write early in the research process and that you write something regularly. Learning about what kind of writer you are is a process discussed in Chapter 5.

Project management

Organizing a research project is certainly no worse than taking two teenagers and a dog on holiday or organizing a fundraising event. Who needs to be there, what do you need them to prepare, how you will co-ordinate things and when does it all need to come together are key questions in organizing a research project. You may have internalized your ability to ask these questions in your day-to-day domestic and work settings. For research you will need to make explicit your strategies for making things happen.

Critical evaluation

This is the ability to analyse something and see its strengths and weaknesses. It is about not taking something at face value but digging under the surface and seeing what assumptions are being made and what you think about them. People who lead worship regularly say that this is a difficult skill to turn off when you are watching someone else lead worship. Critical evaluation for research is more than being able to say how you would have done something differently, it is about being aware of your assumptions and the assumptions of others.

The value of a research journal

Having a research journal can be a helpful way of writing regularly about your research project in a way that is provisional and allows you to think your own thoughts. It can be a way of working out what you think and seeing how your thinking is developing. The form this takes will need to suit your temperament. Introverts will value a physical notebook or a piece of software such as OneNote for gathering their thinking. Extroverts will be happy to blog or share their journal with peers. Some people work better by dictating their thoughts onto a recorder and then just jotting down bullet points when they replay them. If you are researching practice, it is vital that you have some means of recording and describing that practice so that you can note changes and developments. You need a place in which you can record provisional rather than final thoughts or else you will develop mental indigestion.

What is practice in ministry and mission?

To study practice is to study what we actually do. But we can't study what we do without studying the ideas that shape what we do. For theologians there is the added responsibility of understanding how those ideas relate to the Christian tradition.

Swinton and Mowat helpfully define practice as follows:

> Practices, then, contain values, beliefs, theologies and other assumptions which, for the most part, go unnoticed until they are complexified and brought to our notice through the process of theological reflection. Importantly, practices are also the bearers of traditions and histories. They are not therefore simply individual actions. Rather they are communal activities that have developed within communities over extended periods of time. (2006, p. 20)

A challenge for those studying practice in ministry and mission is to put boundaries around the practice that make the study manageable but do not constrain its full understanding. Practice has pastoral, practical and political dimensions which are related (Cameron 2012). However, the political is often not identified in the pastoral and the pastoral can be overlooked in the political. If the research is to have a critical edge it needs to be open to perspectives that are not apparent on first examination.

How does practice relate to theology?

We think that there is a growing diversity of understandings of the relationship between practice and theology. This is to be welcomed as it shows the fruits of a wider range of people undertaking research in practical theology and bringing their understanding of how God is revealed in human existence to bear. However, it does highlight the need to be clear about the assumptions informing your research and to discuss them with your supervisor. Sometimes different assumptions that haven't been explored can lead to 'talking past each other' and leave you with an uneasy feeling that your research is 'not on the same page' as your supervisor. This section offers a preliminary classification, but we feel this is a conversation starter which others need to evaluate critically.

Correlational approaches

For some practical theologians, action and reflection are inseparable – there are no actions that are not shaped by ideas and there are no ideas that do not result in action. For these theologians the challenge is to become aware of the relationship between belief and action by correlation – that is comparing the two. Practical theologians taking this approach would differ in the relative authority given to the Christian tradition in relation to practice. So for example, Swinton and Mowat (2006) propose that the Christian tradition should 'baptize' the social science methods used in research and so have a greater authority than practice. Stephen Pattison (2000) has advocated a dialogue of equals in which the Christian tradition may be brought under question by lessons from practice as well as the other way round. Two prominent practical theologians, Elaine Graham and Duncan Forrester, have used the metaphors of excavating the sources and norms of Christian tradition in practice (Graham 2002) and mining for fragments of the Christian tradition that may shed a light on practice (Forrester 2005).

These metaphors suggest a more tentative, although no less significant, role for the Christian tradition in a plural society. They suggest that the Christian tradition cannot expect to dominate the discussion.

Empirical approaches

Some practical theologians have taken an approach to research which parallels the approach of the natural sciences. The key exponent of this 'empirical' approach is Johannes van der Ven, a Roman Catholic Professor of Practical Theology in the Netherlands (1990). The researcher identifies a problem he wishes to investigate by looking for where faith in God is manifest as praxis. A hypothesis is formed about the way things are in the life of the Church. Qualitative data is gathered and analysed inductively to understand the dimensions of the problem. Key concepts from this understanding are operationalized into variables that can be tested in quantitative research, often in the form of surveys. This data is analysed deductively to test the hypothesis. A final evaluative phase links the results back to the initial problem in order to make recommendations.

A key UK exponent of this approach is Mark Cartledge, who in his research monograph *Testimony in the Spirit* has undertaken a detailed analysis of a Pentecostal congregation (2010). Other examples would include *The Bible and Lay People* (Village 2007).

Ethnographic approaches

This approach seeks to provide a 'thick description' of practice as a result of an extended period of observation and participation in a community of practice. It acknowledges the significance of context for theology and the importance of description as a theological task (Browning 1991). Ethnography is often used in congregational studies when the researcher wants to do justice to the complexity of the situation (Scharen and Vigen 2011). What the researcher observes and how she records it are affected by her own theological formation and the questions she brings to the study. This means that the written report can raise questions about whose interpretations of theology are fused to form the text. Mary McClintock Fulkerson (2007) in her *Places of Redemption* works at a high level of reflexivity and distinguishes between the thoughts of the participants and the theological interpretations that are triggered for her by her participation in the life of the congregation. This way of studying the Church has generated a transatlantic network, Ecclesiology and Ethnography Network, whose first publication sets out different views on the challenges of relating ethnographic description to theology (Ward 2012). Mary Clark Moschella has developed ethnography into a pastoral practice which feeds back to congregations the results of skilled listening for their theological reflection (2008).

Four voices approach

This approach has emerged from the ARCS project, referred to earlier in this Introduction. It sees practice as one of the places in which theology is disclosed. Actions can be bearers of God's grace and so we can learn about God from studying what people of faith actually do – *operant* theology. This needs to be put alongside what people say about what they do, their *espoused* theology. If there is a tension between what people do and what they say they do, they will often turn to the Christian tradition for authoritative guidance – *normative* theology. Different parts of the Church make use of the Christian tradition in different ways. For some the influence will be felt largely through the liturgy, for others it will involve studying the Bible or key texts from the Church's tradition. The fourth voice of theology is the *formal* voice, the work done by academic theologians to understand the tradition. Although presented as four different voices, each voice interpenetrates the others and influences the others. The task of theological research is to bring the four voices into conscious conversation so that all voices can be enriched. *Talking about God in Practice* (Cameron et al. 2010) sets out this approach and worked examples can be found in Cameron 2012 and Duce 2013.

We would encourage you to read one of the authors mentioned in this section as a first step in tuning in to the different relationships between theology and practice that are possible.

In this chapter we have introduced the book and its authors and started to explore some of the thinking that needs to precede the research process. The questions below are for you to reflect upon as you start to make decisions that will shape your research.

Key decisions after reading the Introduction

- What is my purpose in reading this book?

- Why do I want to do research?

- Why have I decided to undertake this course of study (if applicable)?

- Start my research journal by noting down examples of how the transferable skills crop up in my ministerial work.

- Write an initial description in my research journal of the area of practice I wish to examine and how I wish to develop that practice.

- Choose an example of research I am going to read to stimulate my thinking about how I understand the relationship between practice and theology.

I

What Makes for Good Research?

This chapter offers some ideals to aim for. This contradicts the general approach of the book, which is to be realistic rather than idealistic. We want to help those people who learn best by starting with an overview and getting some idea of what the finished project might look like. The chapter begins by offering six criteria for good research and then urging you to familiarize yourself with the criteria for dissertations for your degree at your university. It then offers a six-point plan which gives the key stages in completing a research project. A sample outline of contents for a Masters dissertation is offered to give a sense of the shape of the finished article. The chapter then moves on to talk about practical theology as interdisciplinary and what it means to work in dialogue with other academic disciplines. Finally, an initial guide to the writing on research methods is offered.

Defining good research

When we brainstorm with students on what makes for good research, the following six criteria come up repeatedly.

- *Relevant* – Will this research topic sustain your interest? The research phase of a part-time Masters degree will typically take up to one year; a part-time doctorate can take five or six years. It is worth thinking about whether your topic will still be of interest to you and to the ministry and mission of the Church in that time. One way of testing this is to ask those who are interested in your practice for their reactions to the topic. Does it pass the 'So what?' test? Does it have potential to influence practice?

- *Feasible* – Have you got the time and the resources to do the research in the way you propose? Can you get permission to talk to the people you want to about the topic? Usually researchers need to reduce the size of the topic and the data gathering to make it manageable. The experience of your supervisor on what is feasible is valuable.
- *Credible* – Will the data collected be adequate to support the claims you wish to make in answer to the research question? Will it build upon what others have found out before about this topic? The amount of data you need to satisfy an examiner may be less than that required to bring about a shift in policy. You may need to use your dissertation research to make the case for a larger piece of research.
- *Reflexive* – Are you able to recognize your starting point in relation to the topic and then actively seek out other views and reflect upon your responses to them? You can't assume that your examiners will share your assumptions. You need to be able to articulate where you are coming from and engage positively with other viewpoints.
- *Ethical* – Have you taken into account the rights and feelings of those who will be affected by your research and those who will be asked to take part in it?
- *Original* – This is only an issue for those doing a doctorate. Each doctoral programme will have its own definition of what it expects by way of originality. This definition needs to be firmly grasped when comparing your research question with the results of your literature review. Have you identified a gap in knowledge about practice which your research will fill?
- *Well-managed* – If you manage your research project in a methodical way, it will be evident in the way in which you write it up. This book is written for people who have other things to do as well as their research, and so it proposes a sequence of steps, which, if followed, can save time and avoid looping back to do things that should have been covered earlier.

A good way to test your understanding of these criteria is to take an example of published research and see how it does, or doesn't, meet these criteria. When groups of students do this exercise as 'homework' and then compare notes, they are encouraged by the fact that published research doesn't always meet all the criteria nor does it always have adequate explanations of its approach.

These days all degree programmes have a manual which sets out detailed criteria about what the university expects the finished piece of research to contain.

Normally some or all of the following will be included:

1 A clear statement of the topic and justification of its choice.
2 A research question and a research design that will address it.
3 An adequate review of relevant literature.
4 An understanding of the methodology and choice of appropriate research methods.
5 Clear presentation of the data.
6 Analysis of the data with substantive conclusions relating to the research question.
7 Evaluation of the research with strengths and weaknesses identified.
8 Proposals for impact on practice and ideas for further research.

These criteria need to be absorbed at the beginning. The most effective exercise is to take an example of a dissertation written for your degree at your university and skim read it using the criteria for your degree. How do you think the candidate meets the criteria? You will no doubt discover both strengths and weaknesses. But the fact it is in the library means that it is both a finished dissertation and one that passed – so take comfort that what you produce is also likely to have strengths and weaknesses.

Degree handbooks really come into their own when you have completed a first draft of your dissertation and start to edit your work. Do for yourself what the examiner will need to do and check that all the criteria have been covered. It often needs only a few paragraphs to draw out the way in which you have met a particular criterion.

The other thing to bear in mind is that these criteria are non-negotiables. Some researchers struggle with the idea that the criteria won't be altered to suit their interests or to avoid things they find difficult. A Masters degree and in particular a doctorate are a public signal that you have covered the ground and achieved an acceptable level of competence in all the key skills that research involves. Supervisors vary in the bluntness with which they insist on the non-negotiables, but, in the end, they will have done you no favour if you get to the examination stage and find that you have missed a criterion. The examiner is left with nowhere to go – they cannot pass a piece of work that lacks a vital element.

Institutions vary in their requirements – it is your responsibility to read the manual and return to it when necessary. Do not rely upon your supervisor's memory of it – they may not have noticed small changes from year to year. Make sure you have the correct version for your course and year. To be blunt, at the end of the day it is your degree, so read the manual.

A six-point plan for a finished dissertation

If you are looking for a pragmatic and workable route through your research, I offer you this six-point plan. I have used it with Masters and doctoral students when I am planning my own research.

Step 1 Topic and research question (Chapter 3)

- Identify a topic that interests you but one that is manageable.
- Find a research question that others might want to know the answer to.

Step 2 *Literature review (Chapter 5)*

- Keep accurate notes of bibliographic data and page numbers of quotes.
- Don't finalize your research question and design until you've read the literature.
- Work out what disciplines and fields you are engaging with.
- Write up the literature review.

Step 3 *Methodology and methods (Chapter 7)*

- Design the research carefully – getting a good match between research question and methods.
- Be aware of your methodological approach – are your methods an appropriate match?
- Negotiate access to your research setting and seek ethical approval – these always take longer than you think they will.
- Write the methodology chapter in draft.

Step 4 *Data collection (Chapter 7)*

- Become competent in any methods you intend to use.
- Pilot any method, such as interview schedule or questionnaire, to iron out the bugs.
- Plan a clear timetable for data collection and don't get distracted.
- Don't worry if things go wrong – you'll need some interesting weaknesses for the methodology chapter.

Step 5 *Data analysis (Chapter 7)*

- Work through your data methodically.
- Reread your literature review – have your views changed as a result of collecting the data?
- Reach some conclusions about your data – but you'll need cooking time to see the ideas emerge from the data.

Step 6 Writing and editing (Chapter 9)

- Start with a title, clear structure and draft abstract.
- Don't be afraid of writing or talking just to work out what you think.
- Build in time for editing once your supervisor has seen a completed first draft.
- Don't lose marks through carelessness – build in time for checking.

Ideally you should have a supervision meeting at the end of each step so you can check with your supervisor that you are on course and have completed that step to their satisfaction. You can then plan with them for the next step. If you haven't completed the work for that step, then reschedule your supervision meeting. There is little point meeting to discuss what you haven't done unless you are totally stuck.

There are two crucial questions that you and your supervisor should ask repeatedly. For Steps 1, 2 and 3 keep asking, 'What am I really trying to do here?' For Steps 4, 5 and 6 keep asking, 'So what? What am I making of this?'

My top tip for avoiding having to go back and do work again is to make sure your supervisor is entirely satisfied with your work at Steps 1, 2 and 3, before you move on to Step 4. In fact, if there was one tip in the whole book I would encourage you to take to heart it is: don't move on to Step 4 until Steps 1, 2 and 3 are completed to your supervisor's satisfaction. I have been close to tears examining dissertations that wobble like a house of cards, because the foundations have been dug after the building has been erected.

If you are building a sabbatical into your research plan, then aim to have reached the end of Step 3 before the sabbatical starts. Steps 4, 5 and 6 are the ones that benefit most from time away from your normal responsibilities. A sabbatical can give you time to collect data or to analyse or write up, but not all three.

What the finished dissertation might look like

Your best guide to what the finished dissertation might look like is to spend time in the library reading past dissertations for this degree from this university.[1] Some universities accept a wide variation in the structure of dissertations; others have conventions that they normally expect students to follow. What follows is a generic outline for an interdisciplinary Masters dissertation. It will give you an idea of how the different elements fit together. It assumes that the word length is 20,000 words.

Dissertation outline

Title

Abstract – the label on the tin   300 words

Acknowledgements – (this is not the Oscars)

Chapter 1 – Introducing the topic and locating it   4,000
in the disciplines

Chapter 2 – Review of literature relevant to the   4,000
topic

Chapter 3 – Methodology and methods and ethics   3,000

Chapter 4 – Reporting data   4,000

Chapter 5 – Analysing data and linking it back   4,000
to the literature

Chapter 6 – Conclusions – short and sweet and   1,000
making connections back to the disciplines

Bibliography

Appendices – research instruments used

The details of your outline may differ, but a key thing to note is the symmetry of the outline.

---

1 If these are not in the library, ask your course administrator for examples.

Figure 1: The structure of the dissertation.

Chapter 1 should set the topic in the context of the area of practice you are hoping to influence by your research. It should identify the academic disciplines within which you are working and how they relate to each other. This chapter will include some of the material you have read for your literature review. Chapter 2 is more focused and offers the justification for the topic and shows what other writers have already said about your topic. It focuses the reader onto the research question you intend to ask. Chapter 3 is a technical account of the methodology, methods and ethics of your research, with an evaluation of the strengths and weaknesses of its execution. I imagine the data being poured through the funnel and being shaped by it. In Chapter 4 you present the data you have gathered addressing directly the research question. In Chapter 5 you analyse and discuss that data, setting your analysis in the broader context offered in Chapter 1.[2] Your final Chapter 6 is the Conclusions, which summarize the argument of the dissertation, offer substantive conclusions and show how they fit into the disciplines you selected. The examiner should experience a flow of argument from beginning to end and a shape which starts broad, becomes focused and then broadens again at the end.

It is common to feel daunted by the length of the dissertation, if you have not written one before. However, this is where the advice to do some writing at Step 2 and Step 3 will help you. You will find how difficult it is to fit everything you want to say into these early drafts. This early writing will ensure you don't start the writing up of your dissertation with a blank screen, which induces paralysis. You have something to build upon.

To make matters worse I want to recommend that you consider producing a second shorter document, a report for those people who took part in the research or who have expressed an interest in what you are doing. This report can focus on two things: what you found out and what the implications are for practice. This frees you from trying to write your dissertation in a way that deals both with its academic and practitioner audiences. It also helps to ensure that your research has an impact on practice. At this stage it may be hard to believe, but it will be quicker to write two documents for the two different audiences.

Working across disciplines and fields

What are a discipline and a field?

Academic life tends to be divided into disciplines and fields. It is not a hard and fast distinction but a useful rule of thumb. Disciplines tend to be subjects that have a long pedigree, so for example, theology, natural sciences, history, economics or literature.

---

2 A variation on this is to have two or three thematic chapters that both present and analyse data within the chapter.

Academic life evolves by specializing, and so many disciplines have developed well-recognized sub-disciplines. So theology would recognize specialists in biblical studies, patristics, church history, systematic theology, ethics or moral theology and contextual theologies.[3] However, academic life sometimes makes a synthesizing move and brings a number of different disciplines to bear on a particular field of human activity. Examples that have relevance to practical theology would include: cultural studies, congregational studies, social policy and voluntary sector studies. Social policy, for example, is interested in social wellbeing and involves people with disciplinary knowledge of economics, sociology, political science and anthropology. When a field of study becomes established it often makes claims to become a discipline, as has social policy, with specialist journals, associations, conferences and professorial chairs.

If you are studying for a degree, it is a degree in something – a particular discipline or field. If you do research as part of that degree then your research needs to be set in the context of the appropriate discipline or field. This understanding of the disciplinary context for your research is particularly important for doctorates. It is built up by attending conferences in the discipline, listening to presentations by key academics and keeping up to date with the way in which the discipline is developing. These additional requirements are difficult, if you are studying for a doctorate part-time, but at the end of the day they equip you to face your examiners. It is helpful to discuss expectations with your supervisor, but here are some basic routines that you can adopt. Identify the conference where you will meet most people in your discipline and attend each year. There are usually discount rates for doctoral students. Once you have completed Steps 1–3 in the six-point plan, make a presentation to the conference – there will usually be specific opportunities for doctoral students to do this. Learn from the discussion of your

---

3 The study of ministry (ecclesiology) and mission (missiology) can form part of systematic theology. However, in courses designed to prepare people for ministry they are often taught as subjects in their own right.

work. Identify the academic journal in your discipline most relevant to your work. Read every issue as it comes out, whether the articles or book reviews seem relevant or not. Identify the publishers who are most active in your field and join their mailing list. Looking at their catalogues will show you what new work is being published. As your research project proceeds, you will become increasingly focused on your topic, yet at the end you will need to write something that shows you can put your topic in the context of the major debates in your discipline. The more prestigious the degree programme you are on, the greater the expectation of this breadth as well as depth will be. It seems unfair, but that's the way it is.

Issues in working across disciplines and fields

The normal advice for a Masters or doctoral student would be to avoid working across more than one discipline. This is because it is difficult enough to master your home discipline without drawing in others. There are also potential problems, if your supervisor has not worked across the same disciplinary boundaries. However, as the discussion of practical theology below will demonstrate, it is not possible to avoid working across boundaries in practical theology. So here are a few guidelines to make that cross-boundary working manageable.

The first guideline is to allow the dialogue partner to speak on its own terms rather than co-opt it to your world view. One way of doing this is to read an introductory textbook and note what it says about the assumptions and fundamental ideas of the discipline. Compare and contrast this with your introductory reading on practical theology.

The second guideline is to build on existing points of contact between the disciplines. It is difficult to be the first to open up the dialogue and so you should look for authors who have already done this and note what they say about the challenges of the dialogue. The searching skills mentioned in Chapter 5 will help you find the points of overlap.

The third point is to pay particular attention to what the dialogue partner says about matters of value and authority. Theology is distinctive in the weight it gives to revealed truths and tradition. The natural and social sciences sometimes assume a position of value-neutrality, presenting their findings as free from value judgements. This is something which theology finds implausible and so it may be a point of contention between the disciplines. Many social scientists are interested in challenging this value-free assumption and so can provide a sympathetic dialogue partner for theologians. An example would be the questioning by some economists of the assumption that markets are driven by rational autonomous individuals who make decisions in their own best self-interest (Atherton, Baker et al. 2011).

What kind of discipline or field is practical theology?

Practical theology is the theological study of practice – most likely a practice of ministry or mission, but it could be a secular practice. Practical theology helps answer the question, 'How do I know what I really believe until I see what I actually do?' The practice it studies could be located in the Church (such as a church wanting to study the way in which it undertakes pastoral visitation) or in the world (such as a minister wanting to study their interactions with a local school). The first example is a group of people wanting to study what they do collectively, the second, an individual minister wanting to study their personal practice. A key aim of practical theology is to see how God can be drawn into the conversation about the particular practice in a way that is appropriate and creative and doesn't patronize or baffle those involved.

If I am doing a course in missiology or ministry, am I still doing practical theology? I would argue that you are, because you need to think about how practice can be studied theologically. It may be that missiology or ministry act as your home discipline and practical theology becomes a key dialogue partner guiding your approach to the research.

Practical theology could be viewed either as a sub-discipline of theology or as a field which brings a number of disciplines, including theology, to bear on practice. Whichever way you view it, practical theology is inevitably in dialogue. It is actively interested in world views other than its own in the belief that they will shed light on the human condition. It may not agree with the assumptions on which those other perspectives are based, but it is always willing to have the conversation.

Some practical theology emphasizes the relationship with theology and some the relationship with other disciplines. Identifying who your dialogue partners are going to be is vital in keeping your project manageable. I remember moaning to my doctoral supervisor that I was 'interested in all of it' but then realizing that if I was going to be competent in setting up a dialogue and enabling the dialogue partner to speak in their own terms, I had to limit the number of partners I engaged with.

Hopefully in your search of past dissertations you will find some that manage this dialogue with other disciplines explicitly. If you have not found any yet, you might try skim reading the following books. *Theological Reflection for Human Flourishing* is an attempt to undertake a cycle of theological reflection with a group of ministers (Cameron, Reader et al. 2012). The reflection process runs into problems in engaging with scripture and so there is a discussion about how practical theology relates to biblical theology in Chapter 6. *Participation and Mediation: A Practical Theology for the Liquid Church* brings practical theology and missiology into dialogue with cultural studies (Ward 2008). In the first part of the book the author, Pete Ward, outlines the contribution the different disciplines will make to his argument.

Introducing the literature on research methods

The first thing to say is that this is not the only book you will need to read. This book helps you find your way around the sort of reading you need to do on research methods. It doesn't do the reading for you. There is now an over-abundance of books on research methods and methodology. My basic rule of thumb is to start with thin books and only start reading thicker books if you need to know more than the thin books offer. This sounds rather arbitrary, but like all rules of thumb it will get you started. If you are a doing a doctorate, you should ideally read something in each of the following categories:

- Doing a literature review.
- The methodology you are adopting plus the relationship between practice and theology you are following.
- Each of the research methods you intend to use.
- Approaches to data analysis.
- Writing up your dissertation.

If you are doing a Masters degree, it is good to start with one of the overview books, which should have a chapter on each of the main methods you might use. Most importantly spend a session in the library you are using and find the shelves on which the research methods books are kept. Just browse through the shelves getting an impression of the different types of book that are there and their potential usefulness.

Many research methods books make a distinction between qualitative and quantitative research. Qualitative research uses descriptions and conversations transcribed into text. Quantitative research uses statistics to measure and analyse the things being studied. The assumption in this book is that most researchers will use a qualitative approach. Those wanting to use quantitative methods would need to have statistical training. However, all pieces of research benefit from using descriptive statistics that put your topic in context. Librarians and denominational research departments should be able to advise on what existing statistics could be useful.

Key decisions after reading this chapter

- What criteria for my research are fixed by my course of study?

- When do I want to finish by and so what might a timetable look like?

- Look at some finished dissertations for my course and note my reactions in my research journal.

- Which disciplines or fields could I be in dialogue with? Identify introductory reading.

- Arrange a session in the library browsing through the research methods shelves and start a list of research methods reading that looks useful.

2

Questionnaires

This chapter focuses on questionnaires and their use within faith-based contexts. It looks at the process of survey design and outlines limitations of the method. The chapter ends with a bibliography of suggested further reading.

Introduction to questionnaires

Questionnaires collect information on a particular topic. They provide a cheap and effective way of collecting large quantities of data from a standardized list of questions. Designing a questionnaire involves carefully reflecting upon what sort of data you require, what you want your data to achieve and what techniques you intend to use for data analysis.

Traditionally, questionnaires have been regarded as a quantitative method. Questions are targeted at a carefully sampled population and are designed to collect information which can be analysed through pre-coding techniques and statistical analysis of different variables. This data is quantifiable and allows relationships to be identified between variables. The surveys are designed to be replicable, and to confirm or disprove existing theories. They tend to be located within an objectivist methodology and positivist epistemology (see Chapter 3). See Further Reading on p. 152.

However, it is also possible to use questionnaires to gather qualitative data for an interpretative study. This enables a mixture of closed and open-ended questions to be asked to a larger population sample than is possible through interviews and focus groups. While these responses can be rich in detail for reflection, they can also be harder to analyse. These questionnaires are unlikely to challenge or change people's attitudes in a direct way, but they may stimulate thinking on a particular topic.

Questionnaires can be difficult to design well and analyse effectively. Their success lies in the technical skill of the researcher to present questions in a clear and unambiguous way so that respondents can interpret them and respond consistently.

An annotated checklist for conducting questionnaires

The use of questionnaires in faith-based research raises some specific issues and challenges. This annotated checklist is interspersed with practical reflections from researchers in the field of practical theology who have recently used questionnaires in their work.

Prior to data collection

There are two common pitfalls relating to the use of questionnaires in ministry and mission. First, because questionnaires are the most well-known research method, it is common for people who are new to empirical work to equate 'research' with conducting surveys, without first identifying the underlying theory or theories informing their work and without first thinking through whether this is the best choice of method available to them to answer their research question. The consequence of this is that time is wasted collecting data that isn't used or doesn't relate to the research question.

Second, people are often surprised to discover how much their previous background and experience leads them to gravitate towards one methodological framework or another. This, again, can blind people to possibilities afforded by other methods. Don't be afraid to build on existing skills and experience when the method is a good match. Equally, don't be afraid to experiment with new research methods and methodological frameworks rather than relying on what you think might work from an experience in a different context.

Case study 1

Use of questionnaires in the context of ministry and mission

Below is the account of Andrew Village (2007), who carried out a large empirical study about how ordinary people read the Bible. We shall read more about this study later on. But note his self-awareness about how his choice of methods was shaped by his background experience:

> Before I trained for ordination I had spent fourteen years as a research scientist, studying the ecology of birds of prey. Ecologists are used to having to scrabble about collect-ing information that is hard to come by and that requires statistical techniques to sort out. Wrestling with ways of quantifying and analysing behaviour was in my blood, so it was hardly surprising that I settled for a more quantitative approach. I think this was the right approach. The losses due to simplification are, it seems to me, outweighed by the ability that quantification gives to test relationships and identify causal factors . . . (2007, p. 8)

Identify the sample population

Once you have identified your research question the first thing to do is to locate, and establish links with, your target popula-tion. The way sampling is carried out is central to survey design. Tim May (2001, p. 93) offers a helpful introduction to prob-ability and non-probability sampling depending upon whether you are designing a more quantitative or qualitative study.

Think through practical issues such literacy rates, sensitivity of research topic, and accessibility. How large and representative do you need your sample to be? Will you communicate with respondents by post, over the phone or online? Who are the gatekeepers you need to approach to access an organization's internal membership? Seeking consent from those in authority is important. Such communication enables you to discover, for example, how regularly your target population receives questionnaires as this might significantly affect your response rate.

Case study 2

Lessons learned from a sample strategy used in a faith-based questionnaire

Sue Rodd completed the MA in Ministry at Oxford Brookes in 2011. Her dissertation was an investigative case study in rural ecumenism. She used questionnaires, supported by initial documentary analysis and focus groups, to explore how ecumenical collaboration in a Wiltshire village was perceived by both churchgoers and non-members. The aim of this congregational study was to make ministry and mission in the community more effective. Responses were obtained from 10 per cent of the adult population of the village (144 respondents).

Of particular interest in this study are lessons learned from the chosen sampling strategy. Sue Rodd was keen not to limit the sample to church members, but to reflect wider demographics of the village. Instead of simply distributing forms to every house in the community (which former attempts at village questionnaires indicated would elicit a low response rate), a purposive sampling strategy was adopted whereby respondents were directly approached by someone known to them, as it was thought these people would be more likely to respond positively to a personalized approach. Five focus groups took place. Eight forms were given to each focus group member (26 people in total). They were asked to collect at

---

least five completed forms, from a range of respondents over a period of a month. This 'snowball sampling' was thought to be better than simply opting for the most accessible respondents, i.e. churchgoers. Sue writes: 'The sampling method used is indicative rather than fully statistically valid as a larger survey might need to be, but I believe it to be appropriate' (2011, p. 38). In addition to copies of the questionnaire being available in the participating churches and publicized in the weekly pew sheets, a PDF version of the form was also put on the village website. Collection boxes were placed in the local post office, and in both churches.

However, 'following receipt of an indignant (anonymous) note about the supposedly "exclusive" nature of the survey' (p. 139), Sue Rodd broadened the survey distribution to include posters in the village and hard copies available in the library, post office and churches. Sue concludes: 'with hindsight, it is clear that this should have been done from the start as a matter of principle to ensure a perception of openness and accessibility. In the event, however, the number of additional responses gained was minimal (less than three per cent of the total received)' (p. 39).

This case study illustrates the importance of having a robust and well-piloted sampling strategy, combined with a flexibility to respond constructively to feedback.

Identify key research themes

Once the sample population is identified the next stage of questionnaire design is to sharpen up the key research themes to be explored. This usually involves collecting some preliminary data from the sample group. A multi-method approach works well here, using, for example, initial interviews, focus groups, and documentary analysis. Each of the case studies in this chapter engaged in this preparatory work (Village 2007; Rodd 2011; Caperon 2012).

Questionnaire design

Background information

All questionnaires should begin with a clear explanatory statement about the purposes of the research. They should also include an address and date for return, your policy on confidentiality and anonymity and researcher contact details. Remember that people are giving up their free time to complete this survey and will expect clear instructions for use. One way of keeping track of questionnaires is to allocate a number to each document. It is also worth getting people to write in black ink. Open-ended questions can be hugely disappointing, if they are illegible.

Types of questions

There are different sorts of questions – closed, multiple-choice or ranking questions, and open-ended questions. Some surveys use a predefined list or Likert scale ranging from, for example, 'strongly agree' to 'strongly disagree'. It is best practice to warm people up with generic questions in an opening section of the questionnaire and to leave personal questions until the end. See Case Study 3 below for an example and Denscombe (2010) and Oppenheim (2000) for further reading.

Pilot your questionnaire

A first draft usually has questions that can be misunderstood, as well as instructions that are confusing or ambiguous. Piloting can iron out these problems and improve data accuracy. Be sure to measure the length of time it takes to fill out the questionnaire at this stage too. Questionnaire length depends upon the context of participants filling it in. But in reality twenty minutes is about the maximum time you can expect people to give.

Electronic questionnaires

It is increasingly common to administer questionnaires by sending them as attachments to emails or providing a link to an online survey site. This can reduce costs and speed up completion, but it excludes those without internet access or IT skills. Social networking sites can also be helpful in recruiting respondents.

During the questionnaire

Maximizing response rates

Ways to maximize response rates include the use of a covering letter that motivates, a clear outline of your confidentiality policy and an inclusion of a prepaid return envelope. Design and layout of a questionnaire influences response rates too.

Case study 3

Response rates affected by question types in a faith-based questionnaire

From 2009 to 2011 John Caperon undertook for the Bloxham Project and OxCEPT the first empirical research into chaplaincy in Church of England secondary schools. He began with a number of scoping interviews, followed up by a series of in-depth interviews with chaplains. From these emerged four main themes for further research: the school and employment context of school chaplains; chaplains' understanding of their role and function; their theological heritage and their understanding of their relation to the wider Church. An online questionnaire seemed the ideal means to explore these issues further across the whole school chaplaincy community. The contact database ran to 382 individuals, but this was in all probability not exhaustive.

Given the aim to allow the voice of chaplains to be heard, a questionnaire was constructed which used a range of questioning styles, including attitudinal questions using Likert scales and also free response, sentence-completion questions. The aim was to ensure that despite the quantitative nature of the research instrument – a survey questionnaire – it should produce so far as possible qualitative data. The instrument proved effective, but also flawed – and design was the key issue.

The first section, on the context for the chaplain's work, sought to gather factual information and was in part successful: where a yes/no option was offered in response to a clear question, such as 'Do you have a formal, written job-description?', the outcomes were clear and reliable. However, the dangers of a 'tick all that apply' question, which sought to gather information about 12 aspects of the chaplain's post, became clear when analysing the results. The figures emerging were simply incompatible: chaplains had been confused by a plethora of issues in a single 'portmanteau' question.

A further feature was that respondents 'dropped off' during the course of the questionnaire. All 218 initial respondents completed Section A of the questionnaire, which asked for factual responses to questions about the chaplain's employment. However, Section B, which asked for responses to questions about the different functions of school chaplaincy and invited a personal perspective via a sentence-completion question, was completed by only 173 respondents. Section C, which sought responses on aspects of the theological roots of chaplaincy practice, was completed by fewer still – 165 chaplains; and the final Section D was completed by 160 chaplains, leaving an overall completion rate of 160 out of 218, or 73.4 per cent.

'Drop off' can easily be accounted for, if a questionnaire is felt by respondents to be too long or to involve too much thought or reflection. Clearly, in this case the progressively more time-consuming nature of the questionnaire was a deterrent to respondents. However, those who did respond fully provided very rich data, notably through the attitudinal and sentence-completion questions. This indicated very clearly that a questionnaire may be effectively used to elicit qualitative data of real value to researchers and to the Christian community.

After questionnaire distribution

How to analyse questionnaire responses

There are plenty of good resources outlining techniques for quantitative and qualitative data analysis (Bryman 2012; Oppenheim 2000). Some of these techniques involve computer software. The most important thing at this stage is to keep in mind your research question.

Case study 4

The use of quantitative data analysis in a Bible and lay people study

Andrew Village's (2007) empirically grounded study *The Bible and Lay People* explores how ordinary people in the Church of England interpret the Bible. He statistically analyses data from 404 questionnaires received from 11 Anglican churches across a breadth of churchmanship. 'Ordinary' Bible readers are defined in the research as those who have not received formal training in academic biblical scholarship. The research began with 20 open-ended interviews with people in and around Northampton, where the author was curate. This information focused on key areas of interest to lay people to help shape questionnaire design. The author discovered that 'How do you interpret the Bible?' was too broad a question to elicit meaningful responses. Thus, questions in both the interview and questionnaire were shaped around a test passage, Mark 9.14–29 (focusing on miraculous healing), which could then be compared to people's wider experiences. The piloted questionnaire was designed to measure a variety of variables connected with biblical interpretation. It consisted of five sections with over 200 questions: the test passage; beliefs about the Bible; miraculous healing; general background information and psychological type. Village presents his statistical results in a meticulous way through numerical tables and figures. While not wholly representative of the Church of England, the study sample did cover a sufficiently wide range of people of different traditions, sex, age and educational experience to enable meaningful analysis. For a carefully balanced appraisal of the strengths and weaknesses of this approach see Village, p. 8.

Criticisms of questionnaires

The limitations of questionnaires include the risk of collecting more data than can be used effectively. Also, the data gathered tends to describe rather than explain why things are the way they are. Furthermore, the time required to draft and pilot the questionnaire is often underestimated. So the usefulness of the questionnaire is reduced if preparation has been inadequate. Questionnaires can sometimes assume a certain degree of respondent literacy rates. Some people talk more easily than they write. That's why, as the case studies in this chapter show, many people combine questionnaires with a mixed-method approach.

Bibliography

Useful chapters in generic books

Bryman, A. (2012), *Social Research Methods*, 4th edn, Oxford: Oxford University Press.

A clear introduction to the use of questionnaires in quantitative and qualitative research settings, with chapters on quantitative and qualitative data analysis, computer assisted data analysis packages, e.g. NVivo or SPSS, E-research, and self-completion questionnaires.

Denscombe, M. (2010), *The Good Research Guide for Small-scale Social Research Projects*, 4th edn, Berkshire: Open University Press. See ch. 9.
This contains an excellent overview of when to use questionnaires, and how to design and analyse them. It also looks at their advantages and disadvantages, with useful checklists.

Specific books and articles

Gillham, B. (2000), *Developing a Questionnaire*, London: Continuum.
This short accessible book introduces questionnaire design to novice researchers. It is intended for those doing small-scale research in real-life settings. No previous knowledge of research methods is assumed.

Oppenheim, A. N. (2000), *Questionnaire Design, Interviewing and Attitude Measurement*, London: Continuum.
A university textbook, reprinted nine times since 1992, containing a detailed background to different survey designs and a wide variety of practical examples. The book also includes information on the statistical analysis of data.

The use of questionnaires in practical theology

Astley, J. and Francis, L. (2009), 'Young Vocation to Ordained Ministry: A Qualitative Study', *Practical Theology*, 2(2), pp. 253–67.
This study draws upon quantitative and qualitative traditions of empirical research to explore young vocations to ordained

ministry in the Church of England. It results in rich data from an open ended online questionnaire filled out by 39 ordinands and recently ordained clergy (61 per cent response rate). The study concludes by recommending further research: a replication of the qualitative approach in other dioceses and denominations and by testing the generalizability of the qualitative findings through a quantitative study conducted across a much wider area.

Heelas, P. and Woodhouse, L. (2005), *Spiritual Revolution: Why Religion is Giving Way to Spirituality*, Chichester: Blackwell.

The Kendal project (sociology of religion rather than theology) used three different questionnaires – congregational, holistic and street survey – as part of a mixed-method approach. Their design and distribution were left to the end of the project to allow time to gather relevant questions using the most appropriate language. The use of prepaid envelopes helped to maintain confidentiality. The research sought to extrapolate localized survey data to draw national conclusions. For more details see www.lancs.ac.uk/fss/projects/ieppp/kendal/methods.htm.

3

Asking Questions that Matter: Research Questions, Research Proposals and Ethics

The purpose of this chapter is to start laying the foundations for your research project. Some of the sections in what follows may seem abstract and hard to grasp at first reading. Don't panic: I suggest you make a start on the parts that do make sense and then move on to Chapter 5. When you have read more of other people's research, some of the issues that seemed abstract will hopefully come into sharper focus.

As a practical theologian it is important to take an interest in the assumptions that underpin your research. The first section of this chapter describes the difference between methodologies and methods. The following sections talk you through a sequence of tasks that will ensure your research is well designed. These include thinking about the question your research will answer, designing research methods that will answer the question and writing up your research plan in a research proposal. It will also be important to identify potential ethical problems, decide how to mitigate them and go through the formal process of ethical approval. The final two sections of the chapter enable you to check that two crucial aspects of your foundations are as secure as you can make them. First, that you have developed a project which is an appropriate size. Second, that you are clear about how your research question relates to theology so that your research is theological all the way through.

The difference between methodologies and methods

Methodology is the philosophical approach to research you are taking and methods are the techniques you use to gather the data that will answer your research question. Some methods work better with some methodologies than others, but on the whole, most methods can be adapted to suit your approach.

In the Introduction, you were encouraged to identify the relationship between theology and practice that would inform your approach. This chapter helps you navigate the writing on

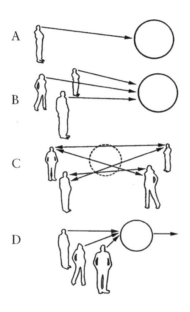

A *There is a real world, and it can be objectively viewed from where I am standing.*

B *There is a real world, but different people will view it differently depending upon where they are standing and what they believe.*

C *Reality is something that is constructed by the interactions between people.*

D *If people want to change what they do, they need a sufficiently shared world view to work together.*

Figure 2: Different world views.

research methodologies. This is a complex topic with different authors advocating different philosophical positions. If you need to delve more deeply, two books by John W. Creswell are helpful in exploring what has been written about methodology: Creswell (2007), in which chapter 2 looks at the assumptions underlying different traditions of qualitative research; and Creswell (2003), in which chapter 1 looks at assumptions underlying quantitative and qualitative research.

This section of the chapter gives a simplified classification of the options and an example to illustrate them. Figure 2 summarizes the different world views that can underpin research.

The table below gives a more complex account of these distinctions using terms found in some writers on methodology.

Methodology	Epistemology	Understanding of theory	Typical methods but not limited to these
A Objectivist	Positivist	Predictive	Surveys, experiments, statistics
B Critical	Critical realism	Subordinate to meta-narrative	Interviews, observation, documents
C Interpretivist	Social constructivist	Heuristic	Interviews, observation, documents
D Action research	Pragmatic	Praxis – theory and practice are inseparable	Action – reflection – action – evaluation cycles including data collection

We will now expand upon the table by using a worked example that deals with each row in turn but uses the same research question: 'Is the local church declining in town X?'

A *Objectivist methodology* defines what aspects of local church life can be measured, gathers statistics, extrapolates trends and reaches predictive conclusions. It may question what the boundaries of the town are and whether behaviour outside the town was affecting church attendance in the town; for example, parents migrating to town churches when their children start secondary school and develop friendship networks in the town.

Books taking this approach are: Jackson, B. (2005), *The Road to Growth: Towards a Thriving Church*, London: Church House Publishing; and Goodhew, D. (2012), *Church Growth in Britain*, Farnham: Ashgate.

B *Critical methodology* identifies 'decline' as part of a controlling metanarrative of secularization and so undertakes interviews and observations to see how local churches accommodate or resist that metanarrative.

A book taking this approach is Brown, C. G. (2009), *The Death of Christian Britain: Understanding Secularisation 1800–2000*, London: Routledge.

C *Interpretivist methodology* asks church members, attenders and non-attenders about their experience of decline and growth. It then sees what data could be gathered to operationalize those different perspectives through interviews and focus groups.

A book taking this approach is Guest, M. (2007), *Evangelical Identity and Contemporary Culture: A Congregational Study in Innovation*, Carlisle: Paternoster Press.

D *Action research methodology* asks key participants in the church what they want to find out about their practices of evangelization. It works with them to develop methods of gathering data, and reflects upon the data and changes practice in the light of insights from the interpretation of the data. The effect of the changed practice in relation to the original questions asked is evaluated.

A book taking this approach is Helen Cameron et al. (2010), *Talking about God in Practice: Theological Action Research and Practical Theology*, London: SCM Press. See an example in chapter 10 of a parish using the Alpha course.

Definitions of what counts as knowledge and theory

Each row of the table takes a different view of epistemology and has a different understanding of theory:

- *Positivist epistemology* takes a dominant interest in precision and consistent research processes. It can accept the need for different perspectives, but overall it is interested in a single clear perspective. There is an interest in using data to build or confirm theory that predicts what will happen in certain future circumstances. The Christian tradition will probably be seen as affirming or challenging the research findings.
- *Critical realism epistemology* embraces pluralism. It emphasizes that everyone is coming from somewhere. Even people who are well disposed towards each other may not see eye to eye and so will need to spend time in dialogue, if they are to act together. Theory is regarded with suspicion as carrying assumptions that may marginalize or silence certain participants. The aim is to critique theory using the Christian tradition as a meta-narrative while regarding that tradition with a mixture of trust and suspicion.
- *Social constructivism epistemology* embraces relativism. If social reality is constructed through the interactions between people, then all value systems are equivalent and need to be tolerated. Theory is merely a tool to stimulate thinking and the asking of new questions. It contains no normative expectations. The Christian tradition will be seen as offering insights rather than a normative basis for discerning right action.

- *Pragmatic epistemology* counts as knowledge that is negotiated between participants and researchers for the purposes of bringing about change. This can come into conflict with a theological concern for the normative, particularly where the research setting does not have a widely accepted understanding of normativity. There is a danger of bypassing the Christian tradition in a search for 'what works'.

By reflecting upon these examples in your research journal you may be able to identify your instinctive approach. Further reading is needed to expand this simplified map of possible approaches. You will need to phrase your research question in a way that fits with the epistemological approach you select.

Research questions, research design

The education system in the UK is better at teaching people how to analyse rather than how to design. Designing research begins with asking a question that matters, being clear about your approach and then choosing methods that are tailored to your approach and will yield data that will answer the question. Good design requires both zooming in on the detail and zooming out so as not to lose the big picture. It involves getting feedback from more experienced researchers than yourself. It is a creative process and so likely to be messy with options discarded as well as adopted. It is easy to be drawn to methods that you feel comfortable with rather than go to the effort of learning new methods that will better fit your research question.

Research questions

This chapter is called 'Asking Questions that Matter' because for people interested in researching practice there is usually an underlying motivation to make a difference. Asking a question that matters to you is also the surest way of sustaining your motivation through the research process.

The point at which the research question is formulated differs between researchers. Some come to the research with a question in mind. Some have a topic they want to investigate but need to do some reading before they can formulate a question. Others need time to develop a hunch into a topic and then propose a question. Inevitably the main question will have spin-off subsidiary questions, but the main question will act as an important focusing tool throughout the research process.

Some books advise students to start with a hypothesis – how they think things are – rather than a question. Hypotheses are used in the natural sciences, where a proposition is advanced and then data collected to try to disprove the hypothesis. This can work well with an objectivist methodology but sits less comfortably with other approaches.

Research design

The key thing in designing research is to ensure that the question is framed in a way that is coherent with the approach and that the methods used are coherent with the question. It is helpful to check out with people how they would respond to a particular method given what you want to find out. So for example, if I am trying to find out about how you feel about something, are you more likely to respond through a questionnaire or through an interview?

It is possible that the question you are asking will benefit from more than one type of data and so more than one method. Some social scientists call this 'triangulation', suggesting that like a map-maker you will be able to measure the height of a hill, if you take three different measurements. There is nothing special about the number three. Different perspectives will add to the richness of your data irrespective of their number. It will normally be time and resources that indicate how many methods you can use.

Identifying key concepts and deciding how they will be operationalized

Don't expect the map to match the territory. In your research journal discuss what the differences are between your key concepts (arising from the literature) and the available phenomena you can observe. See Cameron (2004) for an example of exploring the difference between theoretical concepts and observed realities.

Research proposals

Many universities now helpfully require students to write research proposals setting out what they plan to do. For those of an activist temperament this can seem like yet another hoop to jump through before the 'real' research can start. Having a plan is part of the 'real research', as is getting critical feedback on your plan before you start. The requirements of research proposals vary between universities and courses. The outline below gives you an idea of some of the main areas you need to cover and their significance.

Research proposal outline

- *Title*: the breadth and depth of the topic. Know the rules on titles – if it can't be changed, spend a lot of time thinking about it before submission.
- *Aims of the research*: what you hope the research will achieve – increased knowledge; changes to practice; evaluation of practice; comparison with other contexts . . . If you already have a research question in mind, say what it is or say how you intend to develop the research question.
- *Scope of the research*: it is important to place limitations on the research. These might include disciplinary area, geography, organizational scope, and time period.
- *Rationale*: why the research needs to be done and what gap in knowledge it might fill. If the question has been studied before, are you taking a different approach?

- *Indicative literature review*: what are the main pieces of writing that already exist on the topic? Describe any empirical research that has already been done. Show how your topic will fit into your chosen discipline or field. Indicate which areas of literature you have identified for more detailed review.
- *Indicative methodology*: justify the methodology you intend to use. What assumptions will you be making that will shape your research? What methods might you employ to answer the question? What alternative approaches have you considered and rejected? How will you operationalize key concepts? How do you intend to analyse your data?
- *Timetable*: a timeline for the key stages of the research, paying attention to deadlines from the university and other demands on your time that have to be accommodated.
- *Resource requirements*: any costs or support needs associated with your research and how they will be met.
- *Ethical issues*: either indicate the ethical issues that will be the subject of ethical approval, or complete the ethical approval forms.
- *References cited*: all the references mentioned in the proposal.
- *Indicative bibliography*: references not reviewed in the proposal but which you envisage covering in your literature review.

What is a supervisor looking for when assessing a research proposal?

Here is the checklist I use:

- Topic that passes the 'So what?' test. Will an examiner in one to six years' time see this as a topic that was worth working on and has made a contribution to the discipline/field?
- Builds on at least some previous literature. For a Masters student I would be very reluctant to let them work on a topic

with no previous work to build upon. For a doctoral student this is still a concern, unless they can show why the topic has been overlooked and how other disciplines/fields might have something to contribute.

- Methodology and methods that fit the research question. A research design that doesn't address the question will lead to a flawed project.
- Manageable size. The most common problem is for students to want to tackle topics that are too large or to gather more data than they can report on in the word limit available to them. Narrowing the scope of the research is an important negotiation.
- Ethical problems mitigated. It would be a shame if practical theology didn't tackle ethically complex subjects. Ethical approval processes are to ensure that ethical issues have been identified and potential harms mitigated. It is often possible to redesign a piece of research to reduce ethical risk. This will probably involve dialogue with people who have more experience of designing research.
- In what way is this research theological? Does the topic show the theological significance of the research? Does the methodology include theological methodology?
- Realistic timescale and resource requirements. The course of good research never runs smoothly and so time and resources are needed to deal with the unexpected. Being realistic about timescale and resources can often go hand in hand with reducing the scope of the research.

Research ethics

It is important to scrutinize the research proposal from the perspective of those who will be asked to participate. This section outlines common ethical problems and looks at what is involved in gaining ethical approval for a research project.

Common ethical problems

The key ethical concerns in conducting research in practical theology are that the research does no harm to those who take part, that they understand the purpose of the research and that anything they disclose is treated with an appropriate level of confidentiality. Particular care is needed if you are involving children or vulnerable adults in your research. You will need to check whether the access you require to them makes it necessary to have a DBS (Disclosure and Barring Services) check and whether you need to extend the seeking of consent to their parents or advocates.

A significant challenge of doing research in church contexts is that it is difficult to anonymize the identity either of participants or the research setting, and so there can be reputational consequences, if anonymity is breached. There are real advantages to working with data that people are happy to have in the public domain, and so inviting people to check transcripts of interviews and remove anything they don't wish to see in public can enable their identity and that of the research context to be made known. This is particularly important if the results of your research will be of interest to senior people in the research context.

A vital task of practical theology is to make audible those voices that are usually unheard. Gaining access to these voices requires particular attention to ethics as there are usually reasons why they are unheard. Working with a doctoral student who wanted to access such a group, we came to the conclusion that to contact the group in any identifiable setting was to run the risk of breaching their anonymity. The student therefore decided to work through the administrator of an online support group and offered an online questionnaire that asked nothing about the respondents' context or identity other than checking they were an adult. This opened up a rich seam of data, although it was frustrating not to be able to locate it more specifically in the life of the Church.

Knowing the process and timing for your degree

Ethical approval is one of those areas where your research time-table can be derailed. Universities usually publish timetables, which show how long approval will take, but, of course, if concerns are raised about your proposal, you will need to resubmit, adding further time. Some universities want ethical approval in place before even exploratory conversations about your topic take place; others just want to deal with your main research project. Needless to say, submitting the paperwork correctly filled in to the agreed deadlines is essential to getting the process underway.

Drafting information sheets and consent forms

Some universities wish to see draft information sheets and consent forms and research instruments as part of the ethical approval process; others just want reassurance that such documents will be produced and evaluated by your supervisor.

Information sheets are most helpfully set out as a list of questions and answers about the project for potential participants. They should offer a clear point of contact for participants other than the researcher where they can raise concerns about how the research has been conducted. Where participants have limited reading ability or are working in a second language it is advisable to talk them through the sheet to check for understanding. Consent forms make it clear to the participant what they are agreeing to, including how the data will be recorded and what will happen to those records. Universities often have protocols about how consent forms are to be stored and for how long. See Cameron et al. (2010), appendices 6 and 7 for particular examples, or search university websites for pro formas.

Working with your supervisor

You are most dependent upon your supervisor at the beginning and end of your research. It is worth thinking about how you can bring out the best in each other.

Things supervisees and supervisors want

At the start of working with a supervisor, supervisees often name these as things they want:

- Regular meetings.
- Uninterrupted attention.
- Expertise on content.
- Expertise on process.
- Honest feedback.
- Encouragement.

These seem entirely reasonable expectations, but there are things both parties can do to ensure these expectations are met.

Regular meetings

Meetings need to be booked into the diary, with an agreement as to how long the meeting will last and where it will take place. It is helpful if supervisors set a deadline by which they wish to receive written work, so that they have time to consider it properly before the meeting takes place. Both parties should take responsibility for postponing a meeting where this deadline is missed. There is little point meeting to discuss work that hasn't been done, and it is unrealistic to expect meaningful feedback if the supervisor has not had time to read the work. Students sometimes seek to push at these deadlines, so that the research will fit around other responsibilities they have. Supervisors also have other responsibilities, and they are not thinking about your research project continuously between meetings, so they need time to focus back in on what you are trying to achieve. This is another good reason for having a research proposal which can be an ongoing point of reference.

Uninterrupted attention

It is normal for meetings to take place in the supervisor's office, but some supervisors are better than others at ensuring that they can have uninterrupted time in that space without being distracted by callers, the telephone or what is on their computer screen. Although it takes courage to do so, supervisees should not be afraid to ask, if there is another place or time at which an uninterrupted meeting can take place. Once a relationship is established, video conferencing over the internet can work well.

Expertise on content

If a research project is going well, a student will soon know more about the subject than the supervisor. This can be disconcerting for the student who wants to feel they have the backup of an expert. More helpful is the supervisor's broader knowledge of the discipline or field in which you are working and their ideas about how what you are doing relates to that broader context. Sometimes supervisors can be tempted to 'play the expert' or even worse to co-opt their students' work as their own. Supervisors who generously acknowledge insights from their students tend to be admired.

Expertise on process

Your supervisor's advice about the size of your research project and the different stages of the process will be invaluable. However, this does not mean you should rely on their knowledge of the detail of university regulations. It is your responsibility to find these out and abide by them. If you are working with a novice supervisor, then it is important to take advantage of review meetings where a more experienced supervisor will discuss your progress. You should see these meetings as important occasions for airing any difficulties you are having with the relationship. It is important for supervisors to take advantage of training so that they base their practice as a supervisor upon more than their experience as a supervisee.

Honest feedback

Response to feedback is, for me, the most crucial indicator of whether a student will complete. Being told you are not meeting one of the non-negotiable standards of your degree programme is painful. How you take that on board and respond is crucial. This is where having support to draw upon is vital. Being impervious to feedback puts your supervisor in an impossible situation: they have no choice then but to allow you to learn from failure. Supervisors need to remember there are better and worse ways of delivering bad news. The rules of feedback in any situation apply. Find something you can genuinely affirm and start with that. Be specific in describing what is wrong and offer constructive ideas as to how it can be rectified. Don't put off difficult conversations. Students should enter the examining process with a realistic idea of the strengths and weaknesses of their work.

Encouragement

Most students are daunted by undertaking research; they know they are entering into a process they don't fully understand and where they will need guidance and support. As the previous section suggests, false encouragement is a poor friend. The most important encouragement is that both supervisee and supervisor continue to believe in the value of the research project. It is a brave but important move for a supervisor to say once the research proposal is completed: 'It's a good project, but I don't think I'm the person to supervise it.' Having said that, I have become enthusiastic about topics I didn't initially warm to as a result of catching sight of why they are important to the student.

Locating yourself in relation to your research

The most important help you need from your supervisor at this stage is to develop a project of an appropriate size. This is not your life's work. It needs to be manageable, so you can achieve basic competence as a researcher and then move on and do other things. It is an apprentice piece – showing you have all the skills but not designed to be the best thing you ever produce. If everything you have to say to the world has to be contained in this dissertation, it will never be finished. Drawing

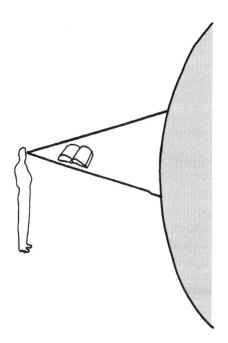

Figure 3: Not my life's work.

your own version of the diagram in Figure 3 may help you reflect upon the type of contribution it is possible to make with this one project and how this dissertation relates to your vocation.

How is this research theological?

Those who are interested in researching practice are often driven by pragmatic concerns such as wanting things they care about to work better. This urge can lead to conducting research that is competent in terms of the social sciences but ends up 'bolting on' some theology at the end in order to satisfy the examiners. This problem can be exacerbated by being taught research methods by a non-theologian or only reading research methods books written by social scientists. Practical theology is an emerging field of study which works on the assumption that practice can be studied theologically. There are no knock-down answers to the relationship between theology and your research, but it is important that you have shown you have thought about the issues and reached some tentative conclusions that then shape the way you conduct your research.

What is the theological question being asked?

The first issue to consider is your understanding of the relationship between theology and practice (see the discussion in the Introduction). Is practice itself a bearer of theology? If so, how is that operant theology disclosed? If practice is seen as not inherently theological, then how will practice be correlated with theology? The second issue is to look at the claims made about practice in the context in which it is being studied. What people say about what they do is significant for the practical theologian because it shapes action. Are those claims about practice a bearer of theology? If so, how is that espoused theology disclosed? If the claims about practice are not seen as inherently theological, then how will they be correlated with theology?

It would be unusual if there were not some differences between what is actually done and what is said about what is done. Should what is done move closer to what is said or should what is said be amended to reflect more closely what is done? It is in resolving these dilemmas that a need to consult the Christian tradition for guidance often arises. Which aspects of the Christian tradition are regarded as especially normative (for example, scripture, liturgy, church teaching) and how is that normativity exercised (for example, interpretation by an authorized person, shared interpretation by discussion between participants, by formation of individuals who then decide)?

It is likely that in handling the Christian tradition the practical theologian will seek insights from those with formal expertise in that tradition. What authority will this formal theology have in reaching conclusions in the research?

Feedback from students is that this 'four voices' approach (Cameron et al. 2010) can be helpful in pinning down more precisely where theology is located in relation to practice, talk about practice and the relationship of both of these to the Christian tradition and academic theology.

Another approach to thinking about the theological content of a research question is to think of Christian doctrine as a grammar that can be used to check the question so it can be comprehended by the Christian tradition (Lindbeck 2009). Practical theology always deals with contextual questions about real situations located within particular strands of the Christian tradition. It is important that research into them engages with that. However, grammar allows people with different dialects to communicate with each other without losing their accent. To give an example, a doctoral student wanted to look at the effectiveness of health ministry in the global faith-based organization he worked for. The pressure from funders was to demonstrate the impact of the health interventions they were funding. A research question about the effectiveness of health ministry seemed appropriate. Inspired by reading Swinton and Mowat (2006), the student experimented with changing the research question into one about the faithfulness of health ministry. This opened up a range of more theological questions about 'faithfulness to what', how mission was understood by the organization, irrespective of the funders' concerns. The process of discerning God's mission in health-care contexts and the relationship of that health care to the life of the local church with its aim of bringing about life in all its fullness became more significant themes in the research. The funders' world view of 'effectiveness' was not dismissed, but it was put in a wider horizon of concerns appropriate to a faith-based organization (Pallant 2012).

Another example would be a group of mothers wanting to look at whether the Messy Church they ran resulted in participants coming to faith. After discussion they reworded the question to 'How does Messy Church help participants turn to Christ?' That rewording allowed a broader interest in the impact that Messy Church was having on them and on those who attended. Their concept of what it meant to 'come to faith' was opened up and their understanding of the difficulties participants had with conventional forms of church was also clearer. They came to understand that Messy Church was about grace overflowing from the life of the church to all who were involved (Watkins and Shepherd 2013).

How will the turn to the tradition take place in the research design?

It is important to be explicit about this in the research proposal.

If a correlational approach is being taken, at what point will the data be brought into conversation with the tradition? Who will be involved in that conversation – just the researcher or a reference group or participants? What method or model of theological reflection will be used and how will its outcomes be written up in the research?

If an empirical approach is being taken, what is the relationship between the data and the tradition? How will concepts from the Christian tradition be operationalized, so that appropriate data will be collected?

If an ethnographic approach is being taken, how will the way in which you write up the research reveal the mark of the Christian tradition on you as researcher and your research context?

If a 'four voices' approach is being taken, how is the discernment of theology in practice and talk about practice understood? Who needs to be involved for that discernment to happen?

A helpful exercise in thinking about how theological reflection will be incorporated into your approach is to look at the two volumes by Graham, Walton and Ward (2005 and 2007). In the first they set out seven different approaches to theological reflection and in the second they offer examples of those models found within the Christian tradition. This could assist with ideas in how to engage with formal and normative sources of theology.

Preparing for your epistemological crisis

Doing research doesn't precipitate a crisis of understanding for everyone. But like any process in which we explore things about which we care deeply, we are likely to be changed as well as change that which we research. This chapter has encouraged you to do some preparatory reading, to talk to your supervisor and fellow students and to use your research journal to record where you think you are starting from. Just being aware of your assumptions can prepare you for the fact that they may be challenged by the research process.

Challenges may come from a number of directions. For example, your understanding of one of your core concepts may be questioned. Your methodological approach may no longer seem appropriate. Your research question may seem to be missing the point in the light of what you have found out.

The key advice is to write down what you think is happening in your research journal and not to despair. Read and talk to people who seem to be where you are now. How did they get there? Keep journaling as your understanding is informed by conversations and reading. A helpful account of how thinking can develop during a doctorate can be found in Ward's (2004) account of her ethnographic research in an Anglican parish.

I've used the term 'crisis' because a change of assumptions will usually lead to needing to take decisions about the direction your research is taking. Hoping that the changes you are experiencing will go away is most likely to lead to writer's block in producing the dissertation. This in turn runs the risk that you will join the ranks of those who don't finish their research. This is where the support you have put in place while you do your research (see Conclusion) needs to be leaned upon as you discuss with your supervisor and others how you should respond.

The good news is that in practical theology, writing reflexively about how your assumptions have changed is seen as a strength rather than a weakness. As an examiner I will warm towards honesty and courage in a carefully described change of direction. I will feel anxious and uncertain when the dissertation seems to be speaking with two different voices that aren't brought into conversation with each other. As Chapter 9 emphasizes, the skill is not in the writing of your dissertation but in your editing of it. If the journey has taken unexpected twists, then signal that in your chapter 1 by giving a brief account of how the project has unfolded.

Key decisions after reading this chapter

- What instinctively do I feel my approach to research is? What reading do I need to do to clarify it?

- What is my first draft research question? Who can I try it out on to get feedback?

- If this is my question and my methodology, what methods would enable me to answer the question?

- What ethical approval procedures do I need to go through and how long will they take?

- Looking again at my research question, am I biting off more than I can chew?

- What can I do to strengthen the relationship with my supervisor?

- Looking again at my research question, can I describe in what way this is a theological question? How will I engage with the Christian tradition?

- Putting this thinking together in a research proposal, what feedback do I get from my supervisor and mentor and how do my plans need amending in the light of that advice?

4

Participant Observation

Armed with the wisdom of my ethnography class, I set off
one Sunday morning in late summer for my debut as a participant observer. My professor, a seasoned anthropologist
with fieldwork in India and West Virginia coal mines, had
an uncanny capacity for 'seeing' the fascinating grain in the
ordinary. Her descriptions of the quotidian were simply poetry.
Now I am eager to emulate her powers of observation and
bring something fresh to theological reflection on ordinary
Christian community . . . (Fulkerson 2007, in the opening of
Places of Redemption: Theology for a Worldly Church)

This chapter accompanies the reader through an annotated
checklist for using participant observation in faith-based
research. It shares experiences from the field and outlines the
limitations of the method. The chapter ends with a bibliography
of suggested further reading.

Introduction to participant observation

Participant observation in a research setting can be carried out in
a structured or more open-ended way. Its purpose is to observe
human behaviour and interaction in its normal setting.

A more structured observation involves a researcher pre-
designing a schedule or checklist of prompts to record what is
being observed in a systematic way. This structured observation can be replicable across settings, the data can easily be

analysed and it encourages the focus to remain upon an over-arching research question.

A more open-ended observation draws upon an ethnographic approach. A researcher immerses herself in the communal or ritual life of a group for a period of time to observe behaviour, listen to conversations and write detailed field notes. If a schedule is used, it is less structured. The researcher's goal is to experience events in the way in which people in the study also experience them, recording not just what people say but also what people do. This data can be rich but harder to analyse. It does not aim to be replicable. Over the past decade, theologians have become increasingly interested in this use of ethnographic research methods to understand religious practice (e.g. Moschella 2012; Ward 2012; Scharen and Vigen 2011).

Participant observers also occupy either an overt or a covert role, the former being most common for researchers in faith-based settings.

An overt role involves the researcher being open about the reason for their presence in the field of study. The researcher is given permission by the group to conduct the research. This allows the researcher openly to record data and the problems of 'going native' are avoided.

A covert role involves the researcher participating fully without informing people of the reasons for their presence, thus the research is carried out secretly. Researchers gain access to groups who might otherwise not consent to being studied. Problems associated with the 'observer effect' are avoided. That said, this method is beset with ethical challenges and there are difficulties for the researcher in taking detailed field notes.

The degree of participation vis-à-vis observation of the researcher also varies enormously. Very often these roles change throughout a course of research. For example, you might start off as a non-participating observer and move into a participating role as your research develops.

Masters students are unlikely to have sufficient time available to engage in an extended period of open-ended observation.

However, a more structured piece of work, driven by a pre-defined research question, can take place over several visits. A doctoral student will have greater flexibility to integrate ethnographic methods into their overall methodology.

The disadvantage of participant observation is that the data rarely provides *reasons* for observed patterns of behaviour. Thus, it is common for participant observation to be used as part of a mixed-method approach.

Annotated checklist for conducting participant observation

Below is a step-by-step guide to carrying out participant observation.

Preparation beforehand

People engaged in ministry and mission are deeply immersed in practice and, in many senses, are already operating as highly effective observers of their surroundings. That said, there are some important issues to think through before becoming a participant observer, especially if the practice you are observing is your own.

Case study 1

Stepping into the role of observer from a context of ministry and mission

Most people are firmly embedded within a *habitus*; e.g. a local faith community, where unspoken and firmly entrenched rules and patterns of behaviour govern the way people practise their faith and the way people judge others. Overfamiliarity with a group can blind an observer to activities taking place. That said, methods of reflective practice such as journaling, supervisions and spiritual direction all nurture skills that enable people to see their practice through fresh lenses,

---

and these skills can be transferable to observing other people. Mellott (2009) describes ethnography as 'a practice of prayerful attentiveness to human beings in their spiritual lives' (in Moschella 2012, p. 228). Moschella (2012) coins the term 'pastoral ethnography' to describe the intentional use of ethnography as a pastoral theological practice. Ethnography, she suggests, is a form of ministry. Questions to reflect upon include: Who is best placed to do participant observation in your selected site? How does familiarity with a context affect your ability to observe? Where might your blind spots be? Careful reflection upon the different roles of practitioner and observer will pay dividends.

Know your research topic thoroughly

A research practitioner should select participant observation as a method, if they think it will provide data that would otherwise remain hidden through other methods. In that sense, there is an emancipatory quality to participant observation. The goal and challenge is to stick to your research question and avoid collecting too much data. A completed literature review will help you identify the most appropriate case-study location.

Access to your research setting

It can be challenging to access an organization willing to let you observe their practices. Participant observation makes people and organizations feel vulnerable, a bit like the arrival of Ofsted or a Mystery Worshipper. There are various means of getting access – asking colleagues, friends and contacts, befriending key people within an organization, providing clear information about your research, offering something in return like a research report or research summary (although do this with caution) and being prepared to compromise if necessary (Bryman 2012, p. 435). Gender can influence access in certain contexts. Once access is granted, a top priority must be building trust and establishing rapport with people.

Develop your participant observation schedule

As already stated, both structured and open-ended observations can use schedules. The aim of a schedule is to reduce the variations that occur through individual interpretation. Predefining your categories will involve a degree of researcher bias, but this is necessary to keep your research focused, especially when data is being gathered from multiple field sites or over multiple sessions involving different observers. It is also possible to develop a schedule from frameworks used by other theologians – see Case Study 2. It is worth piloting your schedule to check that your observations are relevant to the question you are asking.

Case study 2

The development of a methodological framework suitable for observing liturgy

Tracy Robinson is a graduate of the MA in Ministry at Oxford Brookes. Her dissertation was entitled 'Liturgy and identity: what does the liturgy make of me? Interpreting the effect of the liturgy on personal identity in a Fresh Expression of Church'. The study used a social constructivist epistemology, which considers identity to be emergent and contextual. It drew upon the two-stage model for studying the potential after-effects of corporate worship proposed by Stoddart (2005). A schedule was designed that drew upon a model adapted from Catholic theologian Michael Downey's (1997) methodological framework, which sought to study Christian spirituality in a multidimensional and contextual way – exploring influences of culture, tradition, contemporary events, hopes and sufferings, the remembrance of Christ, elements of action and contemplation, charism and

---

community and authentication in praxis (1997, p. 120). This framework also guided data analysis. The second stage of data analysis focused more upon models of identity.

Six consecutive Sunday Eucharists were observed, along with three midweek community meals. Participant observation data was supplemented with texts and images on resource sheets and with song lyrics. The schedule was piloted in another church and amended. It was also decided that data should be recorded in practice *after* rather than during the event, to enable full participation and minimal distraction. Participant observation was followed by semi-structured interviews with the community leader and with another person involved in creating the liturgy. The adaptation of Stoddart's (2005) two-stage model was found to offer an effective research methodology.

During data collection

Be self-aware

On the morning of the observation take note of how you feel at the time. This can influence your field notes. It is good to remind yourself of this when you come to analyse the data. Have your pen and notebook to hand throughout the day and don't be afraid to jot things down.

Case study 3

A word of caution about using a mixed-method approach

It is not advisable to combine two methods at the same time. It was a Friday night. I was in a Church Cold Weather Shelter in North London doing research for a national housing charity. I was principally there to carry out a focus group with volunteers, but given that I was spending the evening at the shelter, I thought it would make sense to combine the task with some participant observation. This was a mistake. First, the imminent focus group was disrupting 'natural' proceedings, and I could sense volunteers were getting nervous. Furthermore, my own frame of mind was not focused upon the skills required to observe. Participant observation requires a whole mindset and warm detachment from activities taking place around you. Make it your sole activity.

Decide whether to observe or to participate

No matter the degree of participation you think you've signed up to do, it is likely that times will arise during your role as participant observer when you will find yourself actively participating in an organizational activity or conversation. The advantage of involvement is that it gives you a greater immersion into the experience. The disadvantage is that it makes it hard to take notes and keep detached. The main thing is to remain self-aware.

Case study 4

The experience of observing in a church-based context

Participant observation in church congregations raises challenges for the researcher, especially in small communities where new people are easily identifiable. Overt researchers operating with the formal permission of a church leadership can still find occasions when people around them are not aware of their role. In these situations a researcher can find themselves operating in a covert role, which can feel uncomfortable. It is a good idea to get information about your research into newsletters or on a poster at the back of the church, and to rehearse explaining your research in a couple of simple, comprehensible sentences.

Some of my own experiences in congregational observation have included: welcome teams enthusiastically shepherding me in the coffee area for the duration of the exercise; the verger off-loading his life history; learning to manage my own over-familiarity with a liturgy, which can be blinding; learning to manage my under-familiarity with a different faith community, e.g. when my guest status in a mosque disrupts the 'natural' setting of a women's religious class. I've also experienced points of tension, when people have been hospitable with both their time and resources, but in the paragraphs of my dissertation I have wanted to ask challenging questions. Keeping a healthy professionalism is important.

Keep an awareness of the 'observer effect'

Two researchers looking at the same event ought to have recorded precisely the same things. Or should they? . . . The powers of observation, the powers of recall and the level of commitment of individual researchers will vary, and this will have an effect on the observational data that are produced. (Denscombe 2010, p. 197)

The way we observe is selective and interpretative. The observer effect is the way in which our presence, our memory and emotions can influence what we record in our field notes. Clearly, the goal is to minimize this as much as possible. My view is that no one can be truly objective.

Case study 5

The observer effect in a faith-based context – Example 1

During a two-year research project at Durham University looking at how young people engage in faith communities across the North East of England, one evening my female Muslim colleague and I visited an Asian youth club. Our gate-keeper was the youth worker, who advised us to join Muslim and Sikh young men playing pool. This was not a success-ful strategy. As we approached, the young people began to drift away. This was an example of the observer effect. Our presence affected the relational dynamics between the young people. The experience raised questions for me about who is best placed to do participant observation. Ironically, we had been seeking volunteers to join an action research team of young researchers, who were to visit other faith-based youth clubs in the area to observe people of their own age.

Case study 6

The observer effect in a church-based context – Example 2

CaFE (Catholic Faith Exploration) is a Roman Catholic orga-nization promoting evangelization through the use of a film, a glass of wine and a small-group discussion. I was invited along by the organizers to observe and participate in a small-group session. Although I was openly welcomed as an overt researcher, it was assumed that I was Roman Catholic, and in a small-group conversation of 'faith sharing' it became dif-ficult to discern at what point to reveal my Anglican identity. Managing this dynamic was distracting. There were ethical questions in my mind about when and how to disrupt the flow of a conversation. When I finally had to disclose my identity, the whole conversation changed course. People were visibly surprised to encounter a stranger in their midst, and this experience revealed deeply entrenched *ad intra*[1] dynamics operating within the Catholic community.

---

1 *Ad intra* refers to the Church's concern with its own faith and order. *Ad extra* refers to the life of the Church in the world.

Participant observation as revelatory in faith-based settings

When participant observation is working at its best, it allows researchers to see a practice with new eyes.

Case study 7

An example of the benefits of participant observation in a church context

An action research project in a Messy Church in South London looked at how to make disciples. A team of leadership mothers took it in turns to observe Monday night sessions. The data added texture to additional interview material. There were some significant 'light bulb' moments and learnings in the data which surprised the leadership team. The team had greater insight into how people experienced Messy Church – their use of space and relationships, which areas of the church were used to send messages on BlackBerries by bored parents, how the sanctuary area was being used by churchgoing children as opposed to non-churchgoing children. Most notably, mothers observed that new parents (unfamiliar with church) participated most attentively in the interactive, Bible story-time at the end of each session. It was the only explicitly 'religious' content throughout the evening, and organizers had assumed this would be the most awkward part for new incoming parents. Prior assumptions of organizers blinded them to the possibility that parents might actually be enjoying themselves. Here practitioner observers were seeing their practice through a critically engaged lens, which uncovered new realities. It was a useful tool for reflective practice for the leadership team of mothers. Story-time now receives more careful preparation by organizers in relation to how this might open up new opportunities to communicate with parents.

After the event

Field notes

Fresh data is best recorded in field notes straight after the event. What is important to remember is that there are no transcripts to fall back on and trigger the memory when you come to write up your research. Your notes are your primary data. This takes discipline and practice.

How to know when to stop observing

Unlike other methods in this book which are one off events, such as a questionnaire or focus group, it can be difficult to know when to stop carrying out participant observation. Usually your research deadlines will determine the parameters of your research. In open-ended observations, you might also find yourself reaching a point of *research saturation*: a moment when you discover that your field notes are repeating themselves, and you feel as if you have a sufficient grasp of the context.

Limitations of participant observation

Most limitations of participant observation are overcome in the context of a multi-method approach. So the fact that observation rarely grasps the intentions behind people's behaviour is corrected by an interview or focus group. The observer effect means that people's behaviour may also change, if they know they are being observed. Data gathered requires careful recording, reading, rereading, coding and analysis to process the material. This can be time consuming and risk oversimplifying a complex reality.

Despite these limitations, this method should offer encouragement to people engaged in ministry and mission. It does not shy away from the realities of church life. Rather, it is dedicated to the collection of material that supports communities of faith in keeping attentive and critically engaged with both contemporary culture and the theological tradition.

Bibliography

Useful chapters in generic books

Bryman, A. (2012), *Social Research Methods*, 4th edn, Oxford: Oxford University Press, ch. 19.
This comprehensive chapter on ethnography and participant observation looks at different ways of gaining access, different roles for the ethnographer, different types of field notes, how to bring the research to an end and the rise of visual ethnography. It is laden with case studies and literature examples.

Denscombe, M. (2010), *The Good Research Guide for Small-scale Social Research Projects*, 4th edn, Maidenhead: Open University Press, ch. 11.
A thorough and engaging introduction to the key features of participant observation, including two helpful checklists.

Specific books and articles

Moschella, M. C. (2012), 'Ethnography', ch. 21 in Miller-McLemore, B., *The Wiley-Blackwell Companion to Practical Theology*, Chichester: Wiley-Blackwell.
This chapter offers a helpful overview of research in the USA and UK that integrates ethnography and religious practice. It introduces a term 'pastoral ethnography' and looks at the relationship of ethnography to other research methods.

Scharen, C. and Vigen, A. M. (2011), *Ethnography as Christian Theology and Ethics*, London: Continuum.
This book looks in depth at the ethnographic turn in theology and ethics. It challenges critiques of the use of social science in theology by Millbank and Hauerwas and demonstrates,

through practical case studies, the use of ethnography in broader fields of theology. Above all, it cautions researchers to recognize their own privilege and bias.

Use of participant observation in practical theology

Fulkerson, M. M. (2007), *Places of Redemption: Theology for a Worldly Church*, Oxford: Oxford University Press.
Theologian Mary McClintock Fulkerson's congregational study uses a cultural anthropological framework, which records rituals, behaviours, kinship relationships and much more than beliefs or ecclesiologically defined practices. It develops a thick description of church life through interviews, Bible studies, meetings and other church gatherings. From this fieldwork come the stories, symbols, habits and patterns that characterize the congregation under investigation.

Ward, F. (2004), 'The Messiness of Studying Congregations using Ethnographic Methods', in Guest, M., Tustings, K. and Woodhead, L. (eds), *Congregational Studies in the UK: Christianity in a Post-Christian Context*, Aldershot: Ashgate.
A valuable reflection upon the ethical and practical problems of a sustained period of participant observation.

Ward, P. (ed.) (2012), *Perspectives on Ecclesiology and Ethnography*, Grand Rapids, MI: Eerdmans.
This book has contributions from 12 scholar-practitioners. It proposes that the Church is both theological and social/cultural, and calls for a methodological shift for researchers in theology. It encourages theologians to utilize ethnographical tools in order to provide more accurate, disciplined research that is situated in real contexts.

Ward, P. and Dunlop, S. (2012), 'Photos reveal what's sacred to young Poles in Britain', research finding summary of

'Migration and Visual Culture: A Theological Exploration of Identity, Catholic Imagery and Popular culture among Polish Young', Kings College London, www.religionandsociety. org.uk/uploads/docs/2012_05/1338216011_Ward_Phase_ 2_Small_Grant_Block.pdf.
An example of visual ethnography whereby young Polish people in the UK took photographs of places that were sacred to them.

Ecclesiology and Ethnography Network, UK and USA
http://ecclesiologyandethnography.wordpress.com/
A network of systematic and practical theologians interested in exploring the interface between ecclesiology and ethnography. They organize colloquiums and publications to advance this field.

5

Finding a Gap in the Field:
Literature Reviews

This chapter addresses one of the most important parts of a research project: the literature review. The main purposes of a literature review are to learn from what other people have already written about your topic, to identify a gap in knowledge that your research will fill, and to design your research taking into account previous research (Hart 1998; Ridley 2004). The literature review can also be used to set the historical or contemporary context for your topic and uncover the main theoretical approaches that have been used in the past. For many researchers the literature review is the first task that raises anxieties about their competence. Surely reading, even if it is a lot of reading, should be straightforward? It is the fact that we have been reading for a lifetime that makes us largely unaware of our habits as readers. We are likely to have habits that are unhelpful, of which sinking into an armchair to enjoy a book is probably the most difficult to overcome! This chapter breaks down the process of doing a literature review into many small steps to help you identify where you need to reflect upon your reading habits.

If you are doing a doctorate, then being able to identify the gap in what has gone before that you are seeking to fill is a key part of demonstrating your originality. If you are doing a Masters degree, it is still important that you acknowledge that you are building upon what other people have done, but the claim to be generating new knowledge is less important. It is more a case of setting the topic in its landscape.

Identifying pools of literature relevant to your question

The first assumption to challenge is that you are going to be able to read everything written about your topic. To start with, you will be limited by the languages you can read and the material you can obtain. Even if your topic has very little academic literature written about it, you are going to have to make your case by looking at adjacent topics, and so you will have to select from them what to read.

A good place to start is with a brainstorming exercise that you share with your supervisor and which ideally you get fellow students to contribute to. The mental image I have is of a cluster of rock pools. At the centre of your diagram place a circle with your topic written in it. The next step is to brainstorm other pools of literature that you think are going to be relevant to your

Figure 4: Rock pools of literature.

topic. They may be from other sub-disciplines and fields that you think will have insights into your topic. They may be aspects of theology that you think are relevant to your topic. You can locate each pool as being close to or further from your topic and also guess its size in relation to your topic. You may already know of overlaps between some of these pools of literature, so represent that on your diagram.

Once you have this visual representation of the task, it may present you with decisions you need to make to ensure your literature review and topic are manageable. For example, if there are both psychological and sociological approaches to your topic, can you deal with them both? If there is a sizable literature from another country, are you going to sample it or set it aside? At this stage, you are working with hunches; the next 'search' stage will enable you to check out those hunches.

Getting feedback on your initial diagram should identify areas of literature that hadn't occurred to you and provide additional insight into the choices you are going to have to make in scoping the literature review. You may have identified disciplines or fields with which you are unfamiliar and you need to decide whether or not it is realistic to enter into dialogue with them. Reading an introductory textbook to the area can help you decide, if this is a subject you will enjoy exploring further. Keep your diagram as a reference point and expand it as you learn more.

Undertaking searches and selecting what to read

Now you have identified your rock pools you can start fishing in them. That is, now you have identified the most significant areas of literature relating to your topic, you can start to undertake searches to see what amount and type of literature is available.

The first point to make is that librarians are helpful people yearning to have meaningful conversations. Your university will have librarians who take a particular interest in the discipline or disciplines you are working in, and there may be a librarian with a particular interest in research methods. Develop your search strategy and then take it to them and ask for advice on shortcuts or additional information sources they are aware of. It is sad that most librarians are rarely consulted for their subject expertise.

Places to search

Library catalogue

Start with the obvious place: the library catalogue of the university at which you are enrolled. Most institutions now have their catalogues online, so you can search at a time and place that suits you. Some even allow you to reserve and renew books online, which means that the time you physically spend in the library can be even better used. If you don't live close to the university at which you are enrolled, you should make every effort to get library access at a library you can get to. Your home university library will help you do this. If you are not registered as a student, see if a theological college will give you temporary library access.

Electronic libraries

One of the significant benefits of being an enrolled student is that you get electronic access to a huge range of resources, of which the most significant for the literature review are academic journals. Not all universities subscribe to every journal, and so if a key journal you need is not included, you need to speak to the librarian. Once you have got used to the different software systems which electronic journals use, you will become adept at scanning the abstracts of articles to see if they look relevant. You should then be able to download the article to read later.

Copyright libraries and Amazon

If you are doing a doctorate, you will need to ensure that no one has done work on your specific topic using your approach.

The catalogue of a copyright library that contains everything published is the first way to do this. However, some copyright libraries are not up-to-date on their cataloguing, and so a check on Amazon is also important, as it usually lists books that will be published in the next six months. To check for other theses on your topic, use the British Library online service called EThOS.

Bibliographies of key books and articles

It should become a reflex when you have read something useful, that you turn to the bibliography and check to see if it contains any relevant items of literature of which you are unaware.

Key classification numbers

As you become familiar with library catalogues you will start to notice that a number of the books that interest you have a similar class mark. It is worth going into the library and browsing all the books with that classification. This may throw up authors of whom you were unaware, particularly people who have gone out of fashion but nevertheless might have something worthwhile to contribute to your thinking.

Be open to serendipity, but it isn't a search strategy. If you wander from one reference to another without a plan, you will lose the big picture. Don't forget to update your searches as you start to write up – the tide keeps coming in over the rock pools, and new things may have arrived.

Personal index of search terms

Electronic searching can both aid and subvert systematic searching. It is easy to build up lists of literature in response to search terms, but it is also then easy to click from one reference to another and lose sight of your original search. If you use bibliographical software, you should be able to download searches and save them, so that you can explore them later and look for overlaps between them.

The best way of being systematic is to keep a list of single words and combinations of words you are using as search terms. Check off when you have used each one in each source you are searching. In deciding on search terms, be aware of common synonyms or differences of spelling or phrase in other key countries. For example, a UK student interested in the children of clergy found that the search term he needed for North American literature was 'pastors' kids'.

Bibliographical information

An advantage of bibliographical software is that you can download references from many catalogues and search engines, saving you the trouble of recording them. Inevitably you will need to record some items yourself. There is a golden rule, which is to take down all the bibliographical information when you have the item in front of you and check it is accurate. Going back at the end of a research project to chase missing bibliographical details adds time and frustration at a stage when you just want to hand the dissertation in. Examiners are expected to read the bibliography and comment on its accuracy. The most common mistakes are missing issue and page numbers for journal articles; missing place of publication; missing edition for second or subsequent editions and inconsistent capitalization of titles.

Bibliographical software is a database that enables you to store, sort, cite and automatically compile bibliographies. For Masters students the size of bibliography is manageable without software. For doctoral students I would strongly urge using bibliographical software. You will engage with more material than you can possibly remember, and so it is helpful to have an electronic annex to your brain where this information is stored and quickly retrievable. There are many advantages. It is searchable. It automates citations and bibliography in the format required by your degree. It can classify your literature into different groups to help you make sense of it. If you use it for keeping notes, those too become searchable. You can record where items are stored. When you become proficient in its use, you can use it for comparing the results of different searches for overlaps, which can help you identify key pieces of literature to focus upon. There are some disadvantages. It will cost you money.[1] Like all databases, if you put rubbish in, you get rubbish out. It doesn't automatically detect and correct your errors. You have to take time to learn how to use it and use it consistently, or else you don't speed up.

Selecting what you will read

You can't read everything. At one level that is reassuring, because the volume of possible reading is vast. At another level that can provoke anxiety, because you may choose not to read something which an examiner later holds up in evidence against you. To avoid that, you need not only to select but to have a rationale for your selection, which you discuss with your supervisor and record in your literature review. You also need to prioritize your reading, so you start with the most relevant and the most recent books and articles. They should contain some element of literature review themselves, and that should start to act as a guide to the literature and highlight other items to prioritize.

As you explore each rock pool, you are aiming to make an assessment of its breadth, depth and relevance to your topic. It may be that a large number of people have reflected upon the topic as practitioners, but no one has conducted any research. It may be that there are a small number of pieces of academic research, but that your research will broaden or deepen what is already known. It may be that someone has already done work on your topic, but that you feel your methodology and methods will offer different insights. You are seeking to make evaluative

---

1 There are free open-source programmes. Check with your library which programmes they support.

comments about the nature and scope of each area of literature as part of making the case for your topic and approach.

For students of practical theology it is common to find that there is little previous academic research on their topic. However, there may be an extensive grey literature. Grey literature is material that has not been produced using academic conventions. Nevertheless it can be important in understanding your research topic or setting the context for it. You need to differentiate between academic and grey literature – practical theologians certainly don't look down on the insights of grey literature, but they will also want to check that they have covered the available academic literature.

It is worth at the outset to check expectations about the volume of reading you will do. This can be done in conversation with your supervisor, but it is also worth looking at dissertations done by previous students on your programme. My rule of thumb is about 40–50 citations for a Masters and about 250–300 for a doctorate, but expectations vary considerably between degree programmes.

Getting hold of literature

'Shopping' is an important and underestimated skill in doing a literature review. Time needs to be built in for doing it. You will need to assemble items from a variety of sources, some of which may be a few mouse clicks away but others of which may require time away from your usual responsibilities. It is a better use of time to have a group of things you need to work on assembled, so you can review them and decide which to focus on, rather than read things in the order you happen to come across them.

Online access

The availability of material online both for reading online and for downloading has improved dramatically in recent years. However, you will need time to build up confidence in using the different databases available, and sometimes there can be frustrations that need to be resolved with a phone call or email to a librarian.

Google Scholar is an important resource, although one that needs to be used with a critical eye as to the provenance of the material. Many universities now encourage academics to put unpublished conference papers, and research reports online. Google Scholar, one of the 'even more . . .' services offered by the search engine, will enable you to locate that material. There is a temptation to rely too much on this material rather than pub-lished material, particularly where library access is inconvenient.

As a registered student you should have a quota of free inter-library loan requests you can make via your institution's library for items it does not hold but which you wish to view. You need to check the timescale for such loans and also whether you will receive hard copy or soft copy.

Visiting the library

Academic libraries can be daunting places full of purposeful activ-ity and complex signage. Most libraries run tours for new users, and this can be the opportunity to identify the subject librarian relevant to your studies. You should also be able to get help in negotiating access to libraries that are more geographically con-venient for you or which contain literature that your university doesn't hold. Getting these access agreements in place early on rather than when you are facing a deadline is advisable.

Deciding how to make use of time in the library is again some-thing that you will develop. For some it will be a rare luxury, for others it will be something they can build into their routine. If your access to a library is occasional, and time is limited, then visits need careful planning, so you focus on things you can only do when you are there.[2] These are usually shopping,

---

2 The online catalogue will enable you to reserve items so they are ready for your visit.

browsing and previewing literature. It should be possible to do your searching and selecting online. The discipline of time in the library can be great for enabling you to preview a number of items efficiently. Using the reading techniques below, take no more than 20 minutes with each item to decide if it is relevant and high or low priority for your topic.

Buying, borrowing and blagging

Electronic bookshops make it easy and tempting to spend a lot of money on books. Having a budget for book purchase can help. Some online bookshops enable you to browse the contents page of a book before deciding whether you need to engage with it further. Second-hand bookshops online can be a helpful way of tracking down older literature on your topic.

It is worth cultivating other cheaper strategies. Many academics and former students have well-stocked libraries from which they are willing to loan to people who have a reputation for returning books. It is good to put a sticky note on the front of the book with the name and telephone number of the person it has come from and the date by which you said you would return it. Open-ended loans are unhelpful in that you are unlikely to engage with the material, and more likely to forget to return it.

It is always worth asking the subject librarian if this is something they would consider buying for the library or subscribing to. They are as keen to spend their budgets as anyone.

Filing

Filing is probably the least glamorous aspect of research but nevertheless vital. When you have gathered literature, you need to know where it is stored. These days that can be in a range of places. You may have a link to an online source, you may have an electronic document you have downloaded, you may have a physical document, or you may have referred to it in a library. Recording the location of everything in your notes is important, if you are going to be able to return to it again quickly without further searching.

I spent a fortune on photocopying when I was a postgraduate student. Now it is possible to photocopy items into an electronic format that is emailed to you. This is cheaper and also makes filing easier.

Effective reading

Becoming aware of your reading habits is crucial to learning to read for academic purposes as opposed to for pleasure. This section suggests techniques for focusing, for reading difficult things and for note taking.

Focusing tips

The first tip can be summarized as 'preview, purpose and pick':

- *Preview*: use the title, contents, index, introduction and conclusions.
- *Purpose*: decide, Why am I reading this? Write down your aim.
- *Pick*: select which bits to focus on.

The second tip is 'review, rehearse and record'.

- *Review*: when you have read for 20 minutes, stop and look back at what you have read.
- *Rehearse mentally* what you have learned in relation to your purpose for reading.
- *Record* that learning.

Reading, like writing, can become blocked. Common reasons include being bored, usually due to loss of focus. Try reading a whole chapter or article at a time, or move away from distractions like email. Other problems are being too tired due to poor posture, lack of breaks or wrong time of day, and trying to read too much due to ineffective selection.

Always carry around the next thing to be read, plus note-taking materials, so you can make use of unexpected down time. If you practise reading in 20-minute blocks, you can make use of a spare half hour.

Reading difficult things three times

Instinctively, re-reading seems like more work, but are you really able to do two or more things at the same time? Not many people can, so it may be easier to break down your reading and note taking of important documents into these three stages.

Reception

- What argument is the author making?
- Is it a claim of fact, value, concept, policy or interpretation?
- What data or reasons are used to support the argument?

Analysis

- What are the strengths and weaknesses of the argument?
- Is it based upon valid evidence?
- Does it make unsubstantiated claims?
- Does it make stated or unstated assumptions?

Evaluation

- How does this argument relate to my research question?
- Does it support or contradict what other writers have said?
- Is it of major or minor significance?

Making notes

It is helpful to have a pro forma for taking notes, so you are consistent in what you record and can compare one item with another. Here are some suggested items for a pro forma.

Memory joggers

- *Date read*: you may read some things more than once, and your opinion of them may change, so you need to see when the notes relate to.
- *Place read*: some people have memories that link what they read to where they were, the weather, what they had for lunch and so on. If this works for you, then make use of it.

Contextual notes

- What discipline or field?
- Who is the intended audience? Academic, student, practitioner?
- What is the purpose of the book or article?
- Is it based upon research?
- If yes, what are the methodology and methods used?
- Who are the key authors the writer relies upon?

If it wasn't useful or relevant, be sure to make a note of why, as you are likely to come across it again.

Reception, analysis and evaluation notes – see above.

Quotes

Get the quote copied correctly first time. You owe it to the person you quote to represent them accurately. Note the page number and other bibliographical data. If you get it right first time, thereafter you just need to cut and paste the quote into your dissertation.

Reviewing literature

The next challenge is to move from the notes you have taken on individual items to a review.

In a literature review you are critically engaging with previous claims that have been made about your topic. If you are taking an objectivist perspective, then you will want to see the evidence for those claims and the warrant for making them. If you are reviewing material written from an interpretativist or social constructivist perspective, you may find that the warrant for making the claim is unclear or not articulated. In theological writing the warrant for making a claim might be scripture, tradition, experience or reason, but that may not be made clear or different warrants may be mixed up. So someone might make a claim based upon a warrant from scripture and then assert that this is also true of experience without backing up that warrant with relevant evidence. So in reading critically it is important to ask what warrant or authority the person is making for the claim as well as the evidence they use to back it up. If this is a new approach to reading, then one way to get into it is to read a chapter quickly and note every claim that is made and then go back and check the warrant for the claim and the evidence produced to back it up. A common fault in theological writing is the unsubstantiated assertion. Another problem is a series of assertions made with different warrants treated as if they are equivalent.

The following sequence of steps can be helpful in constructing your review.

- Take each pool of literature in turn and summarize what the key authors are saying.
- What are the strengths and weaknesses of their arguments?

77

- What are the main areas of agreement and disagreement?
- How do their arguments relate to your topic and question?
- What points of connection between the different pools of literature can you find and what is their significance for your topic?
- What are the gaps in the existing research and how will your topic/question help fill them?

Writing up the literature review

Look at your notes from the reviewing process and identify the most important points you want to make. A good literature review looks like a hand-tied bunch of flowers. There is evidence of selection. The different types of literature are brought together in an arrangement that helps the reader make sense of them. A first draft literature review will sometimes contain only one type

Figure 5: A literature review is like a bunch of flowers.

of flower, and with the student saying that they haven't had time to look at the others – that is to mistake depth for breadth. At other times, a first draft literature review will contain one of every flower in the shop – that is to mistake breadth for depth. There should be evidence both of selection and arrangement. There needs to be a rationale for what has been included and excluded and then a strong sense that the literature is presented in a way that summarizes, analyses and evaluates it. The ribbon tying the bunch together can be likened to the argument that makes a case for your topic and research question.

Set up a draft structure (see Chapter 9 for advice) and identify the authors you will wish to cite and identify in your notes helpful quotations. You will refer to the authors you have read by a mixture of citation, description and quotation. It can be tempting to focus on your own argument and insert citations to suggest that the authors mentioned support it. Citations are better used when you are referring again to someone you have already discussed or drawing in less significant pieces of literature and showing which point of view they support. Knowing how much to describe what you have read is not always easy. You can assume that your examiners are familiar with the core texts of your discipline, but you should not assume they are familiar with disciplines you have brought into dialogue with practical theology or that they have read the specialist literature on your topic. Try to include quotations of no more than two or three sentences that convey the essence of the argument the author is making.

Chapter 9 emphasizes the importance of editing your work. In the writing of the literature review you need to edit your first draft to make it as coherent as you can. You need to get feedback from your supervisor and re-edit in the light of that feedback. You can then set the literature review to one side, knowing that when you come to write up the dissertation it will need to be rewritten in the light of what you have found out in the research. Knowing this may tempt to you move into the research without writing up the literature review. Even if your supervisor wavers, do not give in to this temptation. Just as you will go on to pilot the research methods you will use and learn from the experience, this is your pilot experience as a writer, and what you learn from it will prepare you for later writing. It is difficult to allow the data to change your mind about the literature, if you don't have a clear articulation of what you think before you start the data collection.

When you show your work to your supervisor you need to discuss: Have I shown that there is a gap for this piece of research? Have I shown that I am drawing upon what has gone before in designing what I am going to do? Have I put the topic into context? Have I introduced potential dialogue partners from other sub-disciplines and fields? Have I convinced you this is a work of theology?

It is also helpful to stop at this stage and review with your mentor and supervisor what you have learned about yourself as a learner. Which parts of this process have you enjoyed? Which parts have you found yourself avoiding or putting off? Reflecting upon these may give you insights that will help as the research journey progresses. I use the metaphor of a Stradivarius violin. A player has to learn the unique qualities of each instrument for its true sound to be heard. You are unique, and what you are doing is valuable, and so you have to learn how to get the best out of yourself. I would understand this as part of the co-creative process of being a Christian. You are learning how to draw the best note out and listening to the undertones, because they are part of your development as a life lived to the full.

Decisions following this chapter

- What are the pools of literature that seem relevant to my topic? Which ones am I going to engage with?

- What are my search strategies and how will I select from what I discover?

- If I intend to use new software, how can I become proficient in it?

- From what sources can I access literature and when will this fit into my timetable?

- What am I learning about my reading habits? How do I need to modify them for the purposes of doing a literature review?

- How will I know when I have read enough and can start reviewing my notes?

- Does my literature review make a convincing case for my research topic/question?

- Do I now need to refine my research question and research design in the light of what I have read?

- What have I learned about what I enjoy and put off through the process of doing my literature review?

6

Interviews

We now turn to look at the interview method. There are examples from church-based research and the limitations of the method are outlined. The chapter ends with a bibliography of suggested further reading.

Introduction to interviews

Interviews are one of the most widely used qualitative methods in practical theology. They capture the specific values and meanings an interviewee attaches to a given topic or set of practices. An interviewer's task is to tease out information from an interviewee's experience to explore a predefined research question. It is the interviewer who sets the agenda, designs the questions and makes the final decisions about how to edit and portray a participant's narrative. In that sense, the interview encounter is an unequal one. This power imbalance can be minimized through the establishment of open and transparent channels of communication. An action research methodology can counter this tension by increasing the involvement of participants at each stage of the research process, but this is ill-advised for MA students or people working to tight research deadlines (Cameron et al. 2010).

There is a spectrum of interview styles to choose from depending upon the type of data required by the interviewer and how prescriptive they wish to be about the outcome of the research. These interview styles range from highly structured to unstructured.

The most structured type of interview takes the form of a standardized survey. Here a researcher poses questions that have a number of closed-ended or fixed alternate answers. The analysis of this data allows for systematic and quantitative measurement. This style tends to have its roots in a positivist epistemology (see Bryman 2012).

The most widely employed interview style in practical theology is the semi-structured interview. This is more open-ended. Here the researcher uses a pre-prepared schedule of questions to steer the direction of the interview but in a way that allows sufficient space for the interviewee to shape the ordering and speed of topics covered. This style is more likely to have its roots in a critical realist or social constructivist or action research epistemology.

The least structured interviews are more exploratory in style. They give the interviewee greatest freedom to shape the unfolding narrative. The goal is to capture the uniqueness of the context rather than to attempt to systematize data collected across different interviewees. Examples include life history or oral history methods. This data can be challenging to analyse but rich in 'thick description' of experience for theological reflection.

Annotated checklist for conducting interviews

Below is a step-by-step guide to the completion of an interview, interspersed with case study examples from church-based research.

Prior to the interview

People involved in ministry and mission are well equipped for the task of interviewing. They are familiar with the experience of drawing information out of people in situations of one-to-one encounter in pastoral care, prayer, counselling, spiritual direction and other mission-related activities.

Stepping into the role of interviewer from the context of ministry and mission

Before embarking upon any research, a good research practitioner will reflect carefully upon their role and what is required of them to become an interviewer. This will ensure that when conversations steer perilously close (as they often do in church-based settings) to interviewees seeking theological approval to a given point or a pastoral response, the interviewer will be sufficiently self-aware to resist the temptation to dive in with their advice. As already stated, researchers have permission to set the agenda of the conversation. It is important to be clear with interviewees about the boundaries of any change in role, especially when researchers are already involved in the church or organization (Cameron et al. 2005). If these role differences are not considered, then the integrity, professionalism and authenticity of the research can be compromised.

Research your topic thoroughly

It is important that you know the background to your topic and case organization thoroughly before embarking on data collection. Writing your literature review will sharpen your grasp of the wider issues relating to your topic. Familiarize yourself with the local context and concerns of your chosen case organization(s) before recruiting interviewees. There may be unforeseen activities or sensitive issues taking place in the community at the time of the research that could influence it. This local information will help you design an appropriate interview schedule to make the most out of every interview. Speak informally to as many people as you can, who are familiar with your research site. Think through any ethical sensitivities that may arise and decide how to mitigate them.

Recruit your interviewees

The key task for recruitment is to find out who in your case organization or community has access to the information you require to answer your research question. There are various methods of sampling. Getting a random selection of participants in close-knit faith communities is almost impossible. Snowballing is a common technique used in community-based research, whereby people are recruited in an ongoing way, as new people offer new knowledge that leads to new people (see also Chapter 8 on focus groups for more information about sampling).

If you recruit participants via email, advert or word of mouth, be aware of whom this might exclude. Outward-going, articulate people or parishioners who have their own agendas are easy to attract. Be upfront about what the research will entail and what it can offer. Circulate an information sheet about your research with your contact details to ensure that people are fully informed about the purpose of the research and what will happen to their data.

Remember, for a Masters dissertation you don't need many interviews for your dissertation to be a success. Six to eight interviews will be plenty. For doctorates or practitioner research, be guided by your supervisor and seek a second opinion. Your priority is to articulate to examiners the rationale for your choice and identification of participants and to demonstrate that you have paid sufficient attention to issues of diversity.

If you are reliant upon gatekeepers to recruit participants in whatever context, try to keep attentive to their process of recruitment. They need to be well-versed and trusted intermediaries.

Choose your type of interview

Traditionally, interviews are face-to-face encounters. Telephone and virtual interviewing are beneficial for researchers on a low budget, but they also bring ethical and logistical challenges relating to confidentiality, recording and recruitment. See Bryman (2012) for more details.

Case study 1

Telephone interviews in church-based research

I was invited to carry out some structured interviews for a Roman Catholic youth organization exploring how young people encountered Christ during a national weekend retreat. Rather than disrupt the young people during the weekend itself, it was decided that I should use a short, structured telephone interview three weeks after the event to capture young people's reflections about their experience in the context of ordinary life. It was clear to me that some people opened up more over the phone than in person and others felt more inhibited by the lack of a face-to-face encounter with a researcher. Keeping attentive to these dynamics was important. One disadvantage was that I was reliant upon participants returning a consent form by post.

Prepare your interview schedule

It is advisable to keep questions in an interview schedule clear, focused and simple. Don't dive in with personal or sensitive questions. Start with broad, introductory questions to warm people up and delve deeper into the key issues as the response of interviewees allows. Avoid leading questions that presuppose a particular answer.

Choose your interview venue

Choice of interview venue can impact upon both you and the interviewee in surprising ways. No venue is a neutral place. Churches, homes, public cafés all have their limitations and advantages. It is often logistically easier to allow participants to choose their preferred location for an interview. Questions to reflect upon include: Does the chosen venue (and other people who might be using it at the time of the interview) enable you and the interviewee to feel at ease? Is the chosen venue a safe space and approved by gatekeepers, supervisors and university ethics committees?

Case study 2

Interview venues in church-based research

For my Masters dissertation I interviewed seven co-ordinators of a Churches Cold Weather Shelter serving London's homeless in the winter months. Each interview took place in a different venue at the request of the participant. Venues included: a public café; a participant's church; a participant's home; a participant's office and my own office at Heythrop College. Each venue had a degree of unpredictability, which is characteristic of community-based research. The café got noisy as lunchtime approached. In the participant's home a child was practising the piano in the next-door room. The participant interviewed at work in a central London location moved us twice during the course of the interview due to unscheduled room changes of colleagues. The only time I as researcher had control over the situation was when I conducted an interview in my own office at Heythrop College, but this was an unfamiliar context for the interviewee and may have increased their sense of vulnerability.

Case study 3

Interviewee and interviewer safety in a church-based setting

On another occasion I was interviewing a man at a South London church to explore the impact of the Alpha Course on his sense of belonging to the ecclesial community. I followed university ethical procedures by ensuring my colleagues knew where I was. The vicar beforehand had agreed to let me into the church to use the side room as a venue. Midway through the interview, however, the vicar knocked on the door to say that he had to leave the premises unexpectedly and requested that I turn off the lights and close the door behind me when the interview was over. In no position to change the proceedings, I found myself alone in a church on a winter's evening with a vulnerable adult. It is advisable to check that more people are around in a building at the time of your interview, especially when meeting people for the first time.

During the interview

Prepare the venue

On the day of the interview, arrive early to set up. Shut windows to improve recording quality. Locate spare batteries for the recording device. Remind yourself of the interview schedule and any relevant background details about the interviewee.

Opening the interview

It is good to begin by ensuring the interviewee is comfortable and relaxed. Check that they have read the information sheet. Agree an estimated length for the interview. Get a consent form signed and check the participant is happy for the interview to be recorded, transcribed and circulated for reflection (if appropriate). Remind people that they can withdraw or ask questions at any point, and of the level of confidentiality being offered.

During the interview

A skilled interviewer is a good listener and will know how to draw connections between different parts of the interview. They

will point out inconsistencies and not be afraid to ask for clari-
fication. It is a fine balance to reach between talking too much,
which can make a participant passive, and talking too little,
which can unnerve participants. Denscombe (2010, p. 184)
outlines a helpful list of prompts, probes and checks to use as a
backup, if interviewees get stuck.

Case study 4

People's inexperience of talking about God in practice

A diocesan justice and peace organization asked me to
interview parishioners in a North London Roman Catholic
Church to explore how people connect up the purchase of
fair-trade goods with a spirituality of sacramental living and
the attendance at Mass. Older people in particular struggled
to articulate connections between these deeply integrated
practices – this was despite describing rich practical lives of
social action and ethical purchasing in the local community.
It can be hard to talk to people about their faith, if they themselves have not reflected upon it. It is worth making note of
body language, laughter and moments of prolonged silence
in interviews. These can speak louder than words about how
people are reacting to a given topic.

Case study 5

Touching sensitive issues in church-based research

New mothers attending a Messy Church in a large London
evangelical parish were invited for interview to explore
whether Messy Church was making new disciples. This was
an action research project, which normally entails members of an insider research team (in this case a group of

leadership mothers) conducting interviews themselves. But on this occasion an anxiety was expressed about the impact of interviewing friends on matters of faith, and I was invited to help out as an outside researcher. Their fears proved well founded. The eight participants had no difficulty in talking about their children's faith and their own practical experiences at Messy Church, but when it came to probing about their own faith journey, this was met with defence. Participants' body language spoke volumes. As interviewer I had to juggle between making sure the mothers felt unthreatened and comfortable while also not losing the nerve to push them gently on matters of tension to generate insight. The data collected gave the leadership team much to reflect upon about their practices.

Rounding things off

Pace your interview and watch the clock. Towards the end of an interview it is worth checking that you have people's full contact details for follow-up, such as for checking transcripts or sending out a summary of findings. It is only fair to give participants an indication of your research timetable so they aren't left in the dark about a five-month or three-year gap, or a publication of your intermediary findings in the local newspaper or journal. It may or may not be appropriate to offer to pay travel expenses.

After the interview

Field notes

After the interview, factor in time to reflect upon what went well and what could have been better. How might your own positioning have influenced the participant's responses? This reflection is called self-reflexivity. It's a process that should

underpin your research from beginning to end, looking critically at your practice and keeping attentive to your part played
in the unfolding narrative. Write field notes as soon as you
can when your memory is fresh. Keep a consistent record of
participants' personal information alongside their pseudonyms
to avoid any confusion at a later phase. It can be frustrating
to chase up these details in the final write-up stages of your
research.

Negotiating reflexivity: the issue of faith identity of interviewer and interviewee

Within the field of practical theology it is generally accepted
that interviewer and interviewee may well be 'insiders' of the
same world view and faith tradition. Remaining critically reflective in this context is vital. How much of your identity and values to reveal as a researcher in the process of drawing out an
interviewee is a perennial question – especially when so often
people look for endorsement and agreement before revealing
more about a particular thought process or value judgement in
the area of faith. It is easy to collude in such a dynamic to draw
someone out – yet to what extent does this risk compromising
one's own values? Openness and integrity are usually met with
respect. On the other hand, people can spend the whole interview seeking to work out the positioning of the interviewer if
this dynamic is not addressed. For a discussion of the different
insider/outsider debates in the study of religion and theology,
see Knott (2005).

Transcribing

Data transcription comes in various shapes and sizes. The
universal truth is that this is a time-consuming and laborious
hoop to jump through upon which the success of your thesis
depends. First, it is worth discerning what detail of transcription

is required to fulfil your research requirements. Options range from simply re-listening to recording and making rough notes to producing a full-blown transcript recording every pause, sneeze and 'umm'. Computer packages, such as NVivo, can help you speed up this process, but ultimately this is a long hard slog, unless you can afford professional help. Factor in the time! The greatest challenge in editing, reflection and write-up is to keep faithful to each interviewee's overall narrative.

Limitations of interviews

Interviews can be time-consuming to set up, conduct, transcribe and analyse. They can produce quantities of data, much of which will not be used but requires endless rereading and careful coding to locate the golden nuggets. There are ethical questions to keep in mind about who discerns valid knowledge.

Interviews are limited by the information people wish to share. Some people say what they think you want to hear. Some people's practice may contrast sharply with their words. Some interviewees are less articulate than others. Interviewers are also limited by their own identity and how this is received by the interviewee, for example, gender, occupation, faith. But with adequate sensitivity these limitations can be managed.

Bibliography

Useful chapters in generic books

Bryman, A. (2012), *Social Research Methods*, 4th edn, Oxford: Oxford University Press, ch. 20.
This book introduces different interview styles. It is interspersed with examples from real-life research. It gives advice on how to ask questions and practical tips for recording and transcribing. It also compares interviewing with other methods.

Denscombe, M. (2010), *The Good Research Guide for Small-scale Social Research Projects*, 4th edn, Maidenhead: Open University Press, part II, ch. 10.
This chapter is a user-friendly, concise introduction to interviews. It is thorough and offers practical hints at every stage of the process.

Specific books or articles

Gillham, G. (2000), *The Research Interview*, Real World Research Series, London: Continuum.
This pocket guide to interviewing covers: the nature of the interview; for and against interviewing; developing questions; a really helpful section on different sorts of listening – verbal and nonverbal; use of prompts and probes; piloting and running the interview; and analysis and write-up.

Rubin, H. and Rubin, I. (2005), *Qualitative Interviewing: The Art of Hearing Data*, 2nd edn, Thousand Oakes, CA: Sage Publications.
A more comprehensive, philosophically grounded text that conveys the complexities of analysing interview data. Laden with helpful advice about how to get the most out of each interview.

Examples of the use of interviews in practical theology

Christie, A. (2012), *Ordinary Christology*, Farnham: Ashgate.
This book uses interviews with ordinary Christians to explore their understanding of Christ and salvation.

Heskins, J. (2001), *Unheard Voices*, London: Darton, Longman and Todd.
Using the methodology of contextual theology five selected members of a congregation interviewed a randomly chosen group of parishioners about their views about same-sex couples. Heskins also interviewed a selection of couples who had had their same-sex unions blessed.

7

Reaping What You Sow:
Piloting Methods, Gathering Data
and Analysing Data

This chapter takes you through six steps in executing your research. It should enable you to develop your research plan and ensure you have built time in for each step.

Learning and piloting methods

For many people the research they do for a Masters or doctorate is their first experience of conducting research. Examiners know this and so they are looking for competence rather than perfection. Rather like the driving test, you need to show you are safe to be let loose on the public highway, but the expectation is that you will continue to learn and develop. It is important to record what you learn about the process of research in your dissertation so that the examiner can be reassured that this process of development is underway. Research is itself a practice which can be reflected upon and improved. If you are researching in order to develop or change practice, it is particularly important that the research is executed competently.

Learning methods

People sometimes approach a research project with preconceived ideas that it will involve a questionnaire or interviews and then are surprised when different methods seem more appropriate. Chapter 3 asks the question: If this is my research question and my methodology, what methods would enable me to answer the question? This may have left you considering research methods that hadn't previously occurred to you. The even-numbered chapters in this book aim to introduce you to the pros and cons of the main qualitative research methods, but they by no means exhaust the possibilities.

There are a number of routes into learning a new research method. The most obvious one is to read a number of books that describe the method and then make notes on what existing skills you can redeploy and what further development you might need. For example, you may be used to chairing meetings and so have skills in ensuring that everyone in a group contributes and that decisions are made. The first of these skills transfers to facilitating focus groups, but the second may lead you to over-steer what people are saying. The next step, if you are registered at a university, is to see what short courses it offers in your chosen methods.[1] If this isn't a possibility, then identify a more experienced researcher and see if they will give you a coaching session.

This learning phase can produce a strange mix of feeling both skilled and deskilled. Being aware of the feelings your research methods evoke in you enables you to focus on what you are trying to learn from your pilot study.

Action planning your data collection

I'm afraid I tend to read restaurant menus by starting with the puddings. I need to know how much room to leave for the dessert. That I will have a dessert is never in question. Similarly with a research project, you know you will have to collect

---

[1]   The Social Research Association run one-day courses which non-members can attend: http://the-sra.org.uk/training.

data and so being prepared for that moment and knowing how much space it will occupy in your life is crucial.

In most research projects there are constraints about when and where the research subjects are available and when you are available. An example is the research the ARCS project conducted with a Cold Weather Shelter (Cameron et al. 2010). The Shelter was open between January and March in seven different church buildings, and the guests and volunteers were available late evening. This meant ensuring that all the preparatory work was ready before Christmas and that those doing the fieldwork could get home safely late at night.

It is rare that data collection can be fitted around your existing commitments. You will need to negotiate time out from home and work responsibilities, so you can be at the right place at the right time. It is also important from an ethical point of view, if you are researching people or situations where you are known, that you are clear you are 'in role' as a researcher. It can be tempting to multi-task and tag on some business to the research task, but the danger is you will lose focus and/or confuse people. Build in some contingency time. Even with the best planning, appointments can be cancelled.

Piloting methods

As I have become more experienced as a researcher, I have become keener to pilot the research instruments I have designed. What seems clear to me as a researcher immersed in the topic can be unclear to a research informant who may not have reflected on this issue before. You will need to discard data you gather in pilot studies. This is not extravagant or wasted effort, rather it is an important way to improve the quality of what you produce in the main study. If your pilot reveals problems with your methods, you still have time to change them. A last-minute redesign is better than a failed project.

In situations where there is an existing relationship with informants – particularly if you have a position of authority – it will be necessary to reassure people that you not only want them to engage with the research method but give you feed-back on its strengths and weaknesses.

Another advantage of piloting is that you get a better idea of how long the research will take. People are more likely to cooperate with an interview that really is 45 minutes long than one that asks for 30 minutes but spills over to 45.

Thinking about samples

Identifying how much data to collect and from whom is a key aspect of research design. The temptation is to collect too much data either from anxiety about meeting expectations or because there is always that one last informant who will have the nugget of wisdom you are seeking. Too much data runs the risk that your analysis will lack depth or that you will be frustrated by not being able to write up everything you have done. If your supervisor is experienced, they should be able to help you set a realistic benchmark. If they are not, the most helpful thing is to review dissertations from your course at your university to see how much data has been collected.

Relating samples to epistemology

The rationale for your sample will relate closely to the approach to research you are taking. Chapter 3 outlines four method-ological approaches and the epistemologies that are linked to them. The key question is: Given this approach to research, what sort of sample will be understood as credible? To take each of the four in turn:

- *An objectivist approach* to methodology is linked to a positivist epistemology which is concerned to identify participants who statistically represent the group or population you are studying. You will need to identify what are the key characteristics by which that representativeness is to be determined.

- *A critical approach* to research is linked to a critical realist epistemology which is concerned to get a number of different perspectives on the topic under study. You will need to identify who might legitimately have a view and ensure those views are represented, even if you are not concerned to make that representation statistically valid. A case-study methodology, for example, would want to talk to several people rather than a single informant.

- *An interpretivist approach* to methodology is likely to be linked to a social constructivist epistemology. Which voices do you need to hear from to understand how this shared situation has been constructed? How can you access minority as well as majority voices? Purposively sampling particular stakeholders within a population will be necessary to ensure as many viewpoints are sampled as possible.

- *Action research* usually takes a pragmatic approach to epistemology. It asks how much data and of what kind will be credible to the participants who are seeking to change their practice as a result of what is discovered.

Relevant, feasible, credible

In Chapter 1, relevant, feasible and credible are offered as criteria for good research, and it is worth applying them to sampling.

Criteria for the sample need to be relevant to the question. It is often assumed that demographic criteria are the most important, but it may be more relevant to find out, for example, which type of liturgy participants attend or whether practitioners have or have not taken part in ministerial review.

As has already been mentioned, most people collect too much data. Your sample size and selection criteria need to be feasible. If you sense the project is getting too big for you to handle, you may need to look again at the research question and whether it is too broad. It is common to build comparisons into research, but the more there are, the bigger the sample gets. You may wish to compare different denominations or different types of community, but check it is essential to answering your question.

Finally, the sample needs to be credible. Will it be sufficient and of the right sort to persuade people to change their practice?

Recruiting participants

Having identified who you need to access you then need a strategy for contacting them. The main difficulty in researching practice in church settings is gatekeepers who are too helpful. They may want to ensure you get 'a good turnout' or that you speak to 'the right people', but this can cut across your criteria for sampling. Avoid agreeing to practical arrangements that will inevitably exclude people you wish to contact. A Wednesday evening may be convenient for you and the gatekeeper, but will it exclude parents with young children who you really want to speak to? Even questionnaires can have an inbuilt bias towards those with the skills and time to complete them.

An important judgement to make is the salience of your research topic to those who you want to respond. If they are unsure that the topic is relevant to them or that they have anything useful to contribute, you may need a stage of briefing participants before you recruit them to your sample.

Practical theology often seeks to research issues that are sensitive or whose significance is poorly recognized. Considerable networking can be required to contact hard-to-access groups. There may also be problems when participants fail to respond in significant numbers or provide trivial data. This often requires a significant reappraisal of the methods being used. However, this is learning in itself and can be indicative of the level of trust between the group concerned and the church auspices under which the research is being conducted. It may be necessary to offer a completely confidential opportunity for participants to explain non-response.

Gathering the data – access, confidentiality and recording data

Access

Access always takes longer than you think. It is common for the initial response to be one of enthusiasm that you are interested in what they do. When you try to firm up the arrangements, then the implications of taking part in research are expressed. For example, 'I'm not sure I can ask people to do this' through to 'What will the bishop think if this research does not paint us in a good light?' Access invariably needs two meetings – the first one to sell the idea of taking part in the research and the second to deal with the objections and reservations.

It is common for researchers to accept the confident 'yes' of the gatekeeper. But who else is behind the gatekeeper and what timescales do they work to? 'Perhaps I should consult the church council?' This turns out to be six weeks away. 'But the next meeting is when we approve the budget, and that's always a difficult meeting, so maybe it should go to the one after that.' So that means the researcher is now 12 weeks from getting a decision.

Another difficulty in church settings is for the gatekeeper to urge you to conduct your research informally. Perhaps people already meet for coffee, and you are invited to do your research then or maybe at the end of an existing meeting. It is important to consider if this is likely to yield the quality of data you need. If it won't, then it is better to be honest and negotiate the access you really need.

Confidentiality

It will be the quotations from the data that bring your dissertation to life. It is worthwhile being meticulous about the permission you get from informants, so that you can write up with the confidence that you can quote the data in front of you.

It is tempting to promise people total confidentiality, but in church settings that can be difficult to deliver. Test out any anonymizing strategies as part of your pilot study to see if they work. Don't promise more than you can offer, and whatever you agree, put it down on paper. It is preferable, although more work, to give people the opportunity to correct transcripts so that you are working with material they are happy to have in the public domain. This means you can work with lower levels of confidentiality. In settings where you are trying to change policy and practice that can be especially helpful. If the research topic is too sensitive for that to be possible, then you need to consider contacting people outside the church structures they belong to.

Information sheets and consent forms give you the opportunity to state unambiguously what informants are agreeing to.

Recording data

There are a range of ways of capturing data; these include: face-to-face, on paper or online. Each lends itself to particular equipment and approaches to recording data. You will need to be sure that you can both conduct the research and adequately capture the data. If you are relying on taking notes, check you are able to slow the conversation down, so you really listen to what is being said. If you are using any form of equipment or software, you need to become proficient in its use and confident that, if it fails, you have a backup strategy. If you are using a microphone, will it provide sufficient quality of recording for you to pick up different voices or the emotion in the voice where that is relevant? If you are using free software or online survey sites, will they cope if you have an unexpectedly large response rate?

There is a real sense of satisfaction when you have some data 'in the can'. But you should immediately think about how to make a backup copy. If it is in electronic form, you should ideally have it stored on more than one server.[2] If it is in hard copy, consider whether a spare copy can be stored in another location.

---

2 There are websites that offer this facility for free.

Analysing data

Completing the collection of data is a key milestone in a research project. It can surprise new researchers that they don't automatically know what they think about their data.

Data immersion

Effective data analysis comes from immersing yourself in the data. You may be able to recall the gathering of the data, but to engage fully with it it needs to be turned into a text which you can reread a number of times.

The first task is to turn recorded materials into text and expand notes taken in research settings so they are as full as possible. Transcribing is a time-consuming process with ten minutes of recording taking up to one hour to transcribe, depending upon the level of detail you seek to capture. Some forms of research will require you to note every pause and sound; for others is may be sufficient to summarize what is being said. If you have the financial resources to do it, it can be tempting to pay a professional transcription service. The danger in doing this is that you lose the opportunity for data immersion.

If you have made notes about participant observation, they need to be typed up and expanded to include things that you remember on reflection.

Coding

Having changed your data into text you need to decide what approach you will take to analysis. Working systematically saves time and enables you to learn as much as possible from each reading of the data. Many researchers refer to this as coding.

You will have decided as a result of your literature review if there were ideas or concepts that you wished to explore in the research. To take the example of studying church growth and decline – your reading would have led you to the concepts of membership and attendance as being important. In one reading of the data you could highlight places where you think these concepts were defined or insights into them offered. This is often referred to as deductive coding. You take a concept which you think is generally understood and look for particular instances of it in your data.

The alternative approach is to look for ideas and themes that seem to come up repeatedly as you read the data. This is called inductive or en vivo coding. This approach is often used when investigating a topic with little previous research. You may have developed hunches about your data as you gathered it and want to explore them by looking more systematically through all the data.

You may wish to undertake an additional level of coding that logs your reactions to the data. Your data may contain things you identify with or which give you concerns. It can be helpful to make those reactions explicit when you come to interpret.

A different approach to coding is to focus in your early reading of the data on moments when you felt that you and your respondents were 'on the same page' or something that was said provoked 'laughter of recognition'. Write a note to identify what you think the insight of this moment was. This is an approach which relies more on the disclosures that occur in human interaction than concepts (Cameron et al. 2010).

Whether one of these approaches dominates your analysis or whether they are used in combination, it is important to discover what you are identifying as significant and why (Saldona 2009).

Software, word processors, paper and sticky notes

These days there is some very clever software available to help analyse qualitative data. The coding can be done by highlighting text and assigning it a code. Characteristics of research respondents can be logged and these characteristics linked with codes. Codes can be grouped and separated to test emerging thinking. However, the software can be costly and most people need to go on at least two days, training. If you are doing your analysis without access to other users of the software, it can be frustrating if you don't have immediate support when you get stuck.

It is possible to do analysis by using search and highlighting functions in a word processing package. In the past it was done by cutting up paper with text on it and sticking it on bigger sheets of paper to look for patterns and connections. There is increasing pressure to use software, but it is important to choose a technology you can master.

Whatever technology you decide upon, you need a reliable method for backing up your analysis as you go along. If you are using computer files, ensure they are backed up, ideally on a second server. If you are using hard copy, then take photographs of where you are at the end of each session. Analysis cannot be completed in a single session and so you will want to be able to retrace your thinking.

When it comes to writing up your dissertation and making an argument based upon your data, you will need to be able to demonstrate how the data relates to the argument. Therefore working systematically, one thought at a time and coding as you go along, is going to be quicker and give you a firmer footing for your arguments.

Memos

Data analysis is more than the wielding of a highlighter pen over your data. It is about recording the ideas that occur to you as you are immersed in your data. This is often referred to as writing memos.

The first memos to write are those that define a code you are going to use. Initial clarity about what you are looking for may fade as you see other angles emerging. It is common after a coding session to look back at what you have identified and recognize 'definitional drift'. This is helpful as it may signal the need to write a new definition or to split the code into further codes to pick up the subtle distinctions that evolve.

As a set of codes emerge you may start to see connections between them. This is another cue to write a memo tentatively expressing that link. You may also notice that respondents represented by a particular code have a diversity or commonality that is interesting. Once you have completed your coding you will be able to write some 'compare and contrast' memos exploring the patterns that you see in the codes. If writing memos triggers recollections of the literature, it is good to note them down too.

In rereading qualitative data it is common to come across metaphors or sentences that seem vividly to convey an idea 'in a nutshell'. It is worth highlighting these as they can be helpful in supporting the argument when you write up.

Not losing the wood for the trees

At the point at which a student starts their analysis, I feel as supervisor that I am waving them off for a long walk in a dark wood. I can't go with them; I just look forward to hearing their account of what they have discovered. Most students return saying that they can no longer see the wood for the trees and that they feel overwhelmed by the volume of data, codes and memos.

Pattern seeking

Patterns do emerge from data and answers to your research question do begin to form based upon those patterns. Analysis is first breaking down the data into its component parts but then seeking to make connections and draw conclusions.

The patterns usually result from alternating between zooming in on the trees and then zooming out to glimpse the whole wood. Insights may come when you are doing something different. Be ready to capture them. If you are frustrated, try walking away and doing something different. By now you are the expert on your data, and so, although it may be frustrating that you cannot control when it happens, something will start to make sense. Most people confess to practices their families find strange such as keeping a pen and paper at the bedside, in the car and in the bathroom. It is helpful to write down as much as possible about your tentative conclusions before you re-engage with the literature. This part of the research process can't be rushed and so it is difficult to predict how long it will take.

Theological reflection

An essential part of the analysis is to enact whatever theological methodology you built into the research design. This may involve creating a conversation in your mind between the data and the Christian tradition. It may involve working with others to identify theological disclosures in the data. You are likely to find yourself revisiting the authority that theological ideas are to be given in drawing conclusions. You may have adopted an approach that goes with the grain of that part of the Christian tradition in which the study is located or you may have deliberately tried a different approach. Reflect upon the strengths and weakness of your theological approach so you can record them in the methodology chapter.

Revisiting the literature

This is the moment when you express gratitude to your supervisor for making you write a literature review. Your ideas are already set down with clear links to the sources from which they have come. As you reread your literature review you are looking for things that leap out as either confirming or contradicting what has emerged from your data analysis.

Note anything that you have discovered that seems to confirm or contradict what you have read in the literature. What does your data add to what had gone before? You may need to go back to your notes or even the original books to check out ideas that seem particularly important. They may read differently now.

If more than a year has elapsed since you completed your literature review, you will need to update your searches to find out whether any significant new works have been published that you need to take into account.

Drawing conclusions

Having revisited your literature review and made some notes on your reactions, you are now in a position to write a succinct response to your original research question. This answer will help you build and focus your argument as you write up.

As well as answering your research question you will want to draw some conclusions. These conclusions will discuss the relationship between what you have discovered and the literature. They will attempt to locate what you have discovered in relation to the gap in knowledge you sought to fill and the field in which your study was located. You are likely to have identified some important areas that would benefit from further research. In practical theology it is particularly important to identify the implications for practice.

Having reached some tentative conclusions you need to set them to one side for a few days before coming back and subjecting them to critical evaluation. This is known as the 'So what?' test. How do my answer to the research question and my conclusions add to the understanding of the topic and the development of practice? Then you will need to see if your supervisor feels you have passed the 'So what?' test. Of course, if you haven't, the temptation to panic is huge. All that expenditure of effort and you don't feel you have anything substantive to say. The best way forward is to find fellow students who will discuss your findings with you and retrace your steps back through your written analysis towards the woods to see if you have missed anything.

At the end of the day, the litmus test for a doctorate and an aspiration in any research is that you have made an original contribution. By the end of the analysis process you should have an idea of what that contribution is going to be.

Key decisions after reading this chapter

- What research methods do I need to learn and how will that learning take place? Am I confident in my approach to recording data?

- Have I got an action plan for gathering my data?

- What have I learned from piloting my research instruments and how have I modified them for the main study?

- Have I negotiated access and confidentiality and got the necessary written consents?

- What are my strategies for transcribing, coding and analysing data?

- Have I allowed time to 'get lost in the wood' and 'recover the big picture'?

- How do I react to the literature when I reread my review after the data analysis is complete?

- Have I written down a summary of my answer to the research question and some notes about my conclusions?

- Do my conclusions pass the 'So what?' test?

8

Focus Groups

Through focus groups we have gotten tiny glimpses of worlds that we otherwise do not experience. What it is like to suffer from psychosis? What it is like to live with someone who has severe and chronic depression? What it is like to be a veteran? . . . What it is like for Hmong parents who have to rely on their children to read letters from school, because the parents can't read English . . . Depending on where someone is in the world, he or she see things differently. By carefully listening, we get an image of how other people think and feel and why. (Krueger and Casey 2009, in *Focus Groups: A Practical Guide for Applied Research*, p. xv)

This chapter guides the reader through the process of conducting focus groups in church-based research. It shares stories from the field and outlines some limitations of the method. The chapter ends with a bibliography of suggested further reading.

Introduction to focus groups

Focus groups are about listening. They bring together a group of participants who have a common characteristic in their lives to discuss a research topic. Typically focus groups consist of between six to ten people. The goal is not to reach a consensus. Rather, it is to create an environment in which people feel relaxed enough to share spontaneously their attitudes, experiences and values relating to a given topic. Focus groups can access information not easily shared in one-to-one interviews through people bouncing ideas off each other and sharpening and refining their views in response to others. Once convened, focus groups take on a life of their own. The researcher's task is to listen, facilitate and record the unfolding narrative. It is best not to choose this method if the topic is particularly sensitive or could be harmful to someone if shared in a group. It is also wise to proceed with caution if the topic of discussion is likely to ignite pre-existing tensions within a group who already know each other.

Unlike the in-depth interview where the interviewer has considerable power to shape the course of the conversation, the facilitator of a focus group has less control beyond asking open, probing questions to keep the discussion on track.

Annotated checklist for conducting focus groups

Below is an annotated checklist to help you successfully complete a focus group in church-based research. It guides you through each stage of the process and helps you anticipate the issues and problems that might occur through case-study examples.

Prior to the focus group

Stepping into the role of focus group facilitator from the context of mission and ministry

People working in the fields of mission and ministry are usually inundated with weekly demands to attend groups: Bible study groups, cell groups, community groups, school groups, prayer meetings, social justice groups, music groups, social events and so on. Each group will have an agenda (or lack of it), a style of facilitation (or lack of it) and an expectation about your personal role within it (whether that be acting as chairperson or simply being present at the back). Regrettably, listening is rarely the top priority of church and community groups. But the goal of focus groups is to listen intentionally. Think carefully about which transferable skills you have to support you in your role as focus group facilitator and which skills you might need to develop or refine.

Research your topic thoroughly

As with the in-depth interview, it is vital that you know the background to your topic and case organization thoroughly before beginning to recruit your participants.

Recruitment of participants

The recruitment of focus group participants requires careful discernment of the target audience. Krueger and Casey (2009) term this audience the 'information-rich cases' – those people with the greatest amount of insight on your topic. If your access depends upon the support of gatekeepers, think through whom you can trust and who might be sympathetic and knowledge-able about your research aims.

Qualitative research textbooks write extensively about different styles of sampling, snowballing being the most common method (see Dahlberg and McCraig 2010). But often these fail to acknowledge the extent to which researchers may not have as much control as they would wish. Willing volunteers drop out at the last minute, people don't respond to email and often you find yourself relying upon a committed faithful group who turn up on that cold winter's evening to ensure your research sticks to timetable.

Case study 1

Reasons why people participate in faith-based focus groups

If you do not invest time identifying the most 'information-rich cases', you will find that people turn up to focus groups

---

to take part for all sorts of reasons: 'The vicar told me to come.' 'It was in the newsletter.' 'I write the church magazine and wanted to get a new article for next month.' 'I thought it might help me reflect on my faith a bit more.' 'I have a grudge against this church or vicar or X person and I want to tell you all about it . . .' (or words to that effect!).

There are benefits and limitations of 'piggybacking' upon existing meetings. It can greatly speed up the organizational logistics of setting up a focus group, but there can be pre-existing group dynamics, particularly in close-knit faith communities, which can be hard for an outside researcher to pick up on. Some background research and careful preparation can avoid such pitfalls.

Send participants an information sheet outlining the purposes of your research, and clear directions to the focus group venue. Pilot your focus group question schedule where possible (see below for the best format). It is also worth ensuring there are no significant power imbalances between recruited participants.

Case study 2

How to deal with unexpected visitors in a faith-based focus group

In a focus group with Catholic lay volunteers exploring how people relate homeless volunteering to their faith, I'd left it in the hands of a fellow researcher (and gatekeeper) to access volunteers and to select the most appropriate venue. Everything was going to plan. We gathered in a good-sized room in the Roman Catholic presbytery and were about to start when the Roman Catholic priest walked in and expressed an interest in taking part. My colleague had not briefed the priest about the purpose of the meeting. I knew the priest's presence would impact upon the dynamics of the discussion, but it was difficult for us to refuse the request at that late stage, especially when we were benefiting from his hospitality. The priest's presence acted like a magnet – people looked to him to verify their responses; others I sensed were quieter than usual. On the plus side, his presence meant that he was fully aware of the discussion and had greater scope to effect change afterwards in relation to various issues arising. But thinking through the social role and positioning of participants is really crucial to create an environment whereby people share comfortably and authentically, especially on issues of faith.

During the focus group

Prepare the venue

It is advisable to arrive early to check the venue is prepared. Buy refreshments. Check you have spare batteries to hand. Anticipate any noise or confidentiality issues which might arise.

Case study 3

Anticipate set-up issues in a faith-based setting

A focus group was conducted with volunteers in an Anglican church hall. This hall doubled up as a nursery during the working day. I arrived later than normal to set up and to my surprise the only chairs available were knee height, designed for children. I'd made the error of assuming that chairs of regular stature would be available. As an alternative, I knew that sitting in long rows in pews in the Church next door would close down group interaction rather than open it up. So on this occasion I conducted a focus group of eight people with everyone sitting on small chairs in a circle; an experience outwardly valued by the Quaker in the group! It proceeded well, but had there been older people present, or people with disabilities, this preparatory oversight on my part would have been excluding.

Opening the focus group and establishing ground rules

Ensure people feel comfortable when they arrive. Ask them to sign consent forms, and check they are happy with the activation of the recording device. Repeat an explanation of the research and what you wish to do with the data. Agree a length of the session and try to stick to it. Make time for each person to introduce themselves. It can be helpful to draw a spatial diagram of participants' names to use as an aide-memoire throughout the focus group. Encourage people to speak one at a time.

Case study 4

Whether or not to begin with a prayer

Depending upon the faith tradition of the participants and the topic and context of the focus group, you might find that a group member requests that the group open or close with a prayer. It is not worth dividing a group before you begin, so if this occurs, be sure to have the consensus of the whole group before proceeding. In my experience, a moment of silence for people to use as they wish can work well in this context.

Styles of questions

The facilitator will have prepared a schedule of questions for the focus group. The opening question needs to lead to an easy answer to warm up participants. These responses are not usually analysed. It is worth avoiding questions that highlight power or status differences. These can reinforce insecurities or egos in the group. Next follow questions that encourage the participants to reflect upon their connection with the topic. During these questions participants begin to get a feel for how others view the topic. The central section of the focus group usually entails two to five key questions that drive the study. These questions get to the heart of the issue and are sufficiently open for participants to explore as relevant to them. You need to watch the clock to allow sufficient time to address these questions. The last question brings the focus group to a close and enables participants to reflect on previous comments.

Styles of facilitation

It works well to have two facilitators – one to steer the discussion and one to take notes. Differentiating between multiple voices on a recording can be a challenge. The more that is recorded on the day the richer the data will be. Unspoken data also speaks volumes, as with the interviews; take note of what triggers laughter, silence and variations in body language.

Case study 5

Think carefully about how to facilitate and take notes

It was time for the homeless guests themselves to take part in a focus group. This was facilitated by two researchers. Fourteen homeless people opted to take part – more than the recommended number. Some had limited English. Some may have been under various influences. The discussion was facilitated by a member of an outsider organization who had experience of working with and drawing out responses from the client group. I took notes, observed and interjected with questions from time to time. Facilitating in pairs brings its advantages. In my experience, richer data is retrieved from a shared debrief after a focus group too.

One of the hardest tasks for the facilitator is to ensure that everyone has a chance to speak. Conversations can also easily become 'in-house' or personal – especially if the group know each other and are reflecting back on a community's history or anticipating imminent change. This is where prior research can help you keep up to speed with discussions. Don't be afraid to ask people for clarity and explanations. Be attentive to the fact that new feelings and views can be aired for the first time in these intentional discussion groups. A fine line exists between data gathering and allowing a conversation to descend into gossip, moaning and lamenting.

How to manage people's competencies at speaking about God in practice

People's inexperience of talking about faith can make them passive in focus groups. This is a common challenge across all the methods, the roots of which are explored in Cameron et al. (2010). It is worth at the outset getting groups to articulate their understanding of key words used in your research, such as 'community', 'evangelism', 'mission', 'Church', which all carry deep-rooted assumptions and if not defined early can lead to researchers second-guessing at the write-up phase.

Use materials to stimulate discussion

In focus groups different materials can be used to stimulate discussion on a particular topic (e.g. data from previous focus groups, newspaper clippings, small-group work activity, etc.). This approach, however, needs to be handled with caution to ensure the research question isn't lost.

Case study 6

Use of materials to stimulate discussion in faith-based settings

In a focus group with Catholic parishioners I explored the effectiveness of a Roman Catholic Alpha-style evangelization

---

resource, consisting of a film followed by small-group discussion. During this focus group I facilitated an exercise of getting people to define evangelization and jot down where they thought it was taking place in the parish. This was followed by a richer more focused discussion. This mixed-method approach teased out more information from people and recognized that different modes of communication and pedagogy are preferred by different people.

Rounding things off

At the end of the focus group, check you have everyone's contact details. Agree to circulate research findings and transcripts to those who wish to be informed of the outcome of the research. Thank people for taking part. If you feel the discussion has raised troubling issues for participants, ask them if they wish to discuss them with an appropriate person in the host organization.

After the focus group

Write detailed field notes as soon as possible after the event so as not to lose the detail. Involve participants in reflection upon the data where appropriate. When data has been collected, analysed and written up, be discerning about how best to circulate your work, to whom, in what order and to what timing. If in doubt, go through the powers that be and tread carefully. If the overall aim is to further the mission of the Church and build the kingdom of God, this part of the research needs to be as transparent, orderly and as accessible as possible. Where points of tension are anticipated, talk these through with those responsible before disseminating sensitive findings.

Issues of self-reflexivity

As with the interviews in Chapter 6, discerning whether or not to reveal one's own faith identity as a facilitator in the group is a common question and worth giving careful attention to before the focus group begins. Decide beforehand how much of yourself it is appropriate or necessary to share, and stick to it. Be aware of agreeing or disagreeing with views expressed.

Limitations of focus groups

The number of questions that can be covered in a focus group is limited. Within an hour no more than eight to ten questions can be asked. Words also have their limitations. Participants can intellectualize and not speak from actual experience and practice. Participants may give the answers they think the interviewer wishes to hear and may even make up answers. They can sometimes be reluctant to share emotion and express vulnerability. Furthermore, dominant voices can skew the results. Challenges also arise at the point of analysis relating to interpretation and meaning – How do we interpret other people's words? How do we subject them to rigorous scrutiny? What meaning do we give them? See Bryman (2012).

Bibliography

Useful chapters in generic books

Dahlberg, L. and McCraig, C. (2010), *Practical Research and Evaluation: A Start-to-Finish Guide for Practitioners*, London: Sage Publications, ch. 9.
This chapter demonstrates useful examples of a consent form and interview schedule. It also outlines different approaches to qualitative sampling to identify new focus group participants.

Specialist books and articles

Krueger, R. and Casey, M. A. (2009), *Focus Groups: A Practical Guide for Applied Research*, 4th edn, Thousand Oaks, CA: Sage Publications.
This excellent resource book on focus groups is packed with real-life examples and helpful tips. It goes through every step of the process.

Liamputtong, P. (2011), *Focus Group Methodology: Principles and Practice*, London: Sage Publications.
This introductory text looks at the use of focus groups with vulnerable groups, in cross-cultural research and online. It concludes with a comprehensive chapter on transcribing and analysing focus group data.

Examples of focus groups in practical theology

Cartledge, M. J. (2010), *Testimony in the Spirit: Rescripting Ordinary Pentecostal Theology*, Explorations in Practical, Pastoral and Empirical Theology, Farnham: Ashgate.
Here focus groups are used as part of a mixed-method study looking at the use of testimony in a Pentecostal congregation.

Madsen Gubi, P. (2011), 'An Exploration of the Impact of Small Reflexive Groups on Personal and Spiritual Development', *Practical Theology* 4(1), pp. 49–66.
This research uses focus groups to evaluate the role of reflexive small groups on the personal and spiritual development of ordinands. Six small groups were set up and one focus group. This study highlights the similarities and differences between reflexive small groups (no agenda, begins with a prayer, requires clear setting of boundaries) and focus groups (which have clear, focused questions to explore, tend to be recorded, and transcripts can be sent to participants to validate accuracy).

O'Connell Killen, P. and de Beer, J. (2003), ch. 5, 'Guiding Groups in Theological Reflection', in *The Art of Theological Reflection*, New York: Crossroad.

This chapter gives a useful introduction to anyone wishing to learn how to integrate theological reflection into group facilitation. It offers clear guidelines in the form of 'the five P's': people, purpose, parameters, presence and process. It encourages a deep listening: 'the artful facilitator is the midwife of the movement toward insight' (p. 121).

9

There's No Such Thing as Good Writing: Writing and Editing Your Dissertation

There really is no such thing as good academic writing. No one produces a finished piece at the first sitting. So there should be no fear in writing something, because it can be discarded or improved during the editing stage. Some people need a couple of drafts, others need many. There is no shame or glory in being one or the other. The eventual reader will not be able to detect which you are, if you become effective at editing your own work.

If you have done the writing recommended in this book, you should now have the following documents to hand:

- Your original research proposal.
- Your literature review.
- Your draft methodology chapter.
- Your attempt to answer your research question and draw conclusions.

Backing this up will be all the notes you have made on the literature and all the memos you have written as part of the analysis process. The key benefit is that you are not starting the writing up process with a blank piece of paper.

Making good use of supervision

This is the point in the process where you draw upon the trust you have built with your supervisor. As well as coaching you in effective writing and editing, they should be forming judgements about your work. At the end of the day, you are reliant on them to say when, in their view, the dissertation has reached the appropriate standard.

A good place to start the writing up process is to reflect upon your earlier experiences of writing to consolidate what you have learned so far about yourself as a writer. Which parts of the process do you enjoy, which provoke anxiety, which require dogged persistence?

Only show a chapter to your supervisor when it is as good as you can get it

Once you have agreed a structure submit your writing a chapter at a time or in clusters of chapters. Work at each chapter until it is as good as you can make it. You need your supervisor's feedback on how you need to improve, and it is difficult for them to diagnose difficulties if you don't present the best work of which you are capable.

If your supervisor is happy with the quality of what you are producing, they will encourage you to keep going. Do just that and don't be tempted to stop and re-edit what you have done. There is a danger in being overcritical about what you have produced and so inhibiting the flow of further chapters.

Your response to feedback is crucial. You need to signal how robust you are feeling. Negative feedback on written work can be crushing, so try to meet when you are in a frame of mind to receive. If your supervisor's feedback feels like bad news, summarize and reflect back what they have said to check you have understood it properly. If necessary, do this in writing after the meeting. Putting your head in the sand and hoping for the best are poor strategies for both student and supervisor. Mobilize support, if you are feeling fragile. It is good practice to write up your notes of the supervision session to consolidate what you have learned.

The completed first draft

When your supervisor has read and commented on all your chapters, it is time to produce a completed first draft with contents page, abstract and bibliography. You need to make sure the whole document is coherent and that the argument builds from start to finish. This is a key milestone and time for a modest celebration, without raising your family's hopes that it will soon be over.

Getting feedback on this document is a highly significant moment in the process. This is the first time your supervisor will have truly had an overview of your argument and be able to judge what you have produced as they would if they were examining the dissertation. If you have more than one supervisor, they both need to give substantial attention to this document and ideally meet with you at the same time to agree feedback. If at this meeting substantial reservations are expressed about your work, then ensure you agree an action plan for addressing them. Give yourself time to recover emotionally before returning to the task. If you submit before your supervisor judges your work to be over the line, you will only need to do the work after you have been examined and that depends upon the examiners giving you the opportunity to do so. They may not.

It is becoming increasingly common for doctoral students to ask other people to read this completed first draft; perhaps people who understand the research context or your mentor. You need to be clear about the sort of feedback you are seeking. Is it to help improve the English, or is it to check it is clear to someone who doesn't specialize in your topic or do you want to know if you have done justice to the research setting? If all you want is reassurance, then say so.

The meeting to discuss the first draft is a good moment to discuss suitable examiners if you are doing an MPhil or doctorate. Most supervisors will take your views into account, and through the literature you have read and the conferences you have attended you should have formed views about who might be interested in your work. However, you need to accept that choice of examiners will, for some supervisors, be something that they see as reflecting their academic reputation. They want to draw to the attention of their peers the quality of the work of their doctoral students. So if someone more prestigious than you had in mind is proposed, try to see it as a vote of confidence from your supervisor rather than a cause of anxiety. The advantage of agreeing examiners at this stage is that you have the chance to ensure you have appropriately referenced their work in what you have written. This is also the moment to volunteer for a mock viva, if your institution offers them.

You're on your own

You will have to produce a second completed draft of the dissertation. At the point that your supervisor advises that you are over the line, you are on your own for the final stages of preparing the dissertation for submission. Read the manual, seek advice from the university administrator and attend to all the required details no matter how finicky they seem. If you are preparing a manuscript for publication, you have to conform to the publisher's requirements. This final part of the process is to check that you are able to attend to that level of detail.

Techniques of writing

This section focuses on getting your ideas down on paper; the next section looks at how you edit that into something you are ready to show to someone else.

How do you know what you think?

While I'm suspicious of research that lumps the whole population into two categories, I've come to the conclusion that there are in fact two main categories of writers:

- How do I know what I think until I read what I've written?
- How do I know what I think until I hear what I've said?

For those who work out their thoughts through writing, the temptation is to think that this preliminary writing can be the first draft of the main text. The preliminary writing needs to be regarded as exploratory and as a resource for producing the first draft. For those who work out their thoughts by talking, they need to find sympathetic listeners who will allow them to talk aloud while they make encouraging noises. Afterwards the researcher needs to make notes about what they have learned from their soliloquy. For this sort of researcher, conference presentations and seminars are particularly valuable as their thinking is likely to take a leap forward in the discussion. Build in time immediately afterwards to write down new insights.

Another contrast can be between those who organize their ideas spatially versus those who think in a linear way. Spatial thinkers can feel constrained by a computer screen and need whiteboard and flip charts to sketch out their ideas and the connections between them. Linear thinkers may need to ensure that their writing doesn't read like a list and that they have identified which ideas are more significant than others.

Holding on to the big picture can be a real challenge. Your document in which you state your preliminary answer to your research question may need to act as a guide when you get bogged down.

What conditions help you write?

Writing is such a cerebral activity that it can be easy to ignore the physical human undertaking it and other preoccupations in life imply. Just as with reading, you need to attend to practicalities such as lighting, seating and regular breaks. Displacement activities can be either a useful break or a total distraction from writing up. There are many people who have a finished dissertation and clean kitchen cupboards or a weed-free garden. It is good to be aware of your favourite displacement activities, so you can evaluate whether this is respite or escape. It is also helpful to learn what techniques enable you to set aside daily concerns. For some that is having a 'to do' list handy, so that unfinished tasks that crop up can be noted down rather than distract. I find that having two tables helps greatly. My main table is where I do all my day-to-day work, but I have a smaller table where I do academic writing. Somehow, it is easier to avoid the enticing distractions of bills to be paid and emails to be answered when sitting facing a different wall.[1]

It is also important to learn whether writing on a computer overengages the critical part of your brain. If you are struggling to be creative, it may be easier to start with paper and pen and migrate to the computer when you have your main structure and argument mapped out.

Structure

Most recent word processors include an 'outliner' facility. This is a view of the text that enables you to develop your structure before you start to write. Chapter headings are assigned level 1, sub-headings level 2 and so on. You can promote and demote headings to experiment with their relative significance within the text. You can switch between an overview of the chapters and a detailed view of all the proposed sub-headings. Ideally chapters should be of a roughly even length. You want your examiner to be able to hold the whole structure in their head, so five to nine chapters is a good range to aim for.

If you are writing for a non-academic audience, you need to think about what length of document your audience will realistically engage with and make good use of summaries and layout to guide people to the main points you wish to make. The fewer words at your disposal the greater the challenge you

---

1 Software called 'Self Control' blocks certain activities on your computer for a period of time you specify.

face and the more attention you need to pay to the structure of what you write.

Most people write too much and spend time editing it down. A smaller proportion of people write too concisely and need to expand what they have written when they edit to ensure their line of thought can be followed. If you start by producing a structure for the whole document, you can roughly assign word lengths to each section. This helps you spot problems of over- or under-writing. It may also raise questions about whether you have given too much or too little significance to a particular section.

Knowing where to start

If you have already done the writing outlined at the beginning of this chapter, the logical place to start is with writing the chapters in which you present and analyse your data. These are some of the most difficult to write, and they are the climax to which the dissertation builds. There can often be a debate about whether to present the data and then follow that with a chapter of analysis or whether to identify the major themes in your analysis and present data and analysis together for each theme. What is decisive is what will make it easiest for your reader to follow your argument. Writing is not a neutral activity. What you choose to say and how you say it are shaping the readers' reception of your argument.

For some people the only place to start is at the beginning, and that involves working with existing material to rewrite it to fit the structure you have designed. Set up an electronic filing system, so the various versions of chapters don't become confused.

Techniques of editing

Learning to edit your own work is a crucial skill in writing up research. If you have not had to submit your own writing to rigorous critique before, then it is sensible to warm up by editing the work of others. Take something you read during the literature review, which was interesting but poorly written. What could be done to make this document more readable? Common problems are:

- Sentences that are too long or convey more than one idea.
- Poor links between one set of ideas and the next.
- Assertions without evidence to back them up.
- Technical terms that are not explained the first time they are used.

The challenge of editing your own work is to achieve sufficient emotional distance from what you have written to be critical of it. For most people at least one night's sleep between drafts is necessary to achieve that distance.

The rest of this section focuses on the major issues you need to watch out for when editing.

Introductions, summaries and 'MSM'

Having worked hard on the structure of your dissertation, the chapter headings and side headings convey to you a logical progression in the argument you are making. However, your first draft will probably assume too much mind reading on behalf of the reader in interpreting that sequence of thought. A chapter heading and major side heading signal the need to set out the purpose of the section that follows and at its conclusion summarize what has been achieved. It is difficult to do this during the first draft, and so a key purpose of the second draft is to work out where those introductions and summaries are required and insert them. This increases your word length, which may lead to sacrifices having to be made elsewhere. A useful technique is to think of the end of each section or chapter as changing lanes on the motorway. You look through your rear-view mirror to see where you have been, you signal where you are going next and only then manoeuvre to the next section. MSM or 'mirror, signal manoeuvre' helps maintain the flow of the text. I place this emphasis on flow, because your dissertation needs to pass the Birmingham New Street test. Like many academics I do marking and examining on train journeys, where the opportunities for displacement activities are few. Invariably I change trains at Birmingham New Street, which involves either sprinting for the next platform or taking a break while waiting for the next train. Once settled onto my new train I need to pick up my train of thought. A well-written dissertation will enable me to look at the contents page and then introductions and summaries and so put me back on track. As a student I fantasized about examiners locked in their studies poring over my every word. Now I know the reality. Good topping and tailing not only helps me mark the dissertation but enables me to refresh my memory as I write my report and before I go into the viva. It also means that future generations of students will make use of what you have done, because they can easily locate the parts that are relevant to them.

Editing each chapter

Each chapter needs to be edited so its purpose is clear and it makes a definite contribution to the argument of the dissertation. This section focuses on common problems that occur in chapter editing.

The literature review that you wrote at the beginning of the research process now needs to be rewritten to fit the purposes of the early chapters of the dissertation. In these chapters you will introduce the topic, build the case for the research question and identify and review areas of literature that are relevant. It is evident to the examiner when this rewriting is insufficiently thorough. Check for sections that no longer seem to have a purpose or authors you deal with differently in different places.

A methodology chapter with no interesting strengths and weaknesses arouses my suspicions. I've never done a piece of research that went totally according to plan or where I didn't learn something about the methods I used. This chapter needs to demonstrate your reflexivity as a researcher and your conclusions about the strengths and weaknesses of your approach.

It is common for the writing up of research to have too much data and not enough discussion. To do justice to your topic you may have to deal with less data in order to have the space to discuss it. Conversely, if you overdo the discussion, then your dissertation loses its vitality, because the data is not allowed to speak.

The previous chapter discussed the importance of passing the 'So what?' test. Scrutinize your conclusions carefully to check they are substantive and link directly to your research question.

A final point of scrutiny in each chapter should be excluding over-elaborate footnotes that distract from the main argument. If a point made in a footnote contributes to your main argument, it should be in the body of the text. Having a subsidiary argument running through the footnotes is confusing for the reader.

Having got each chapter to the best place you can and responded to feedback from your supervisor, your task is not over. You now need to check the coherence of the whole dissertation.

Editing the whole dissertation

There is an inevitable desire to give an account of everything you have done. However, the primary purpose of a dissertation is to make an argument for the answer to your research question. You may therefore like a film editor have to face the agony of material that will be left on the cutting room floor. There is no point including every piece of footage shot if the story line will be incomprehensible to the viewer. The precious words you spend on topping and tailing your chapters are words that enable the reader to engage with your argument.

On the front cover of most dissertations is the course or study or the department through which the study has taken place. Sometimes that can be the only real clue as to what discipline the dissertation is contributing too. As discussed in Chapter 1, disciplinary identity in practical theology can be complex. You are likely to be in dialogue with other academic disciplines or fields and will also be drawing on other sub-disciplines within theology. It needs to be clear to what you are making a contribution and how the dialogue with other disciplines and fields has been undertaken.

It is vitally important to avoid the impression that theology has been bolted on to a piece of empirical research that has taken its frame of reference from another discipline. The final part of Chapter 3 discusses how to ensure that your research was theological all the way through. Editing the whole thesis is an opportunity to ensure this is clearly evident to the reader.

Proof reading

I hope I have demonstrated that editing is about a lot more than proof reading. However, proof reading is important. One of the things you are trying to demonstrate is that you can produce material of a publishable standard and that therefore means to the highest standards of accuracy in grammar, spelling, punctuation and layout. It can be good to involve a friend with a track record in accuracy, but at the end of the day you are responsible. Don't forget to proof read the bibliography, paying particular attention to missing items. Whatever punctuation style you adopt for the bibliography, it needs to be implemented consistently throughout.

Writing and editing an abstract

In the exams of your youth, you will have answered questions set by the examiner. In a dissertation you both set the question and provide the answer. It is the title and abstract combined that set the question. They are therefore vital pieces of writing, not afterthoughts. I see the abstract as 'the label on the tin'. The dissertation should then go on to deliver exactly what has been promised. One of the first things I do as an examiner is write down a list of expectations that the title and abstract have set up and then come back at the end to see if they have been met. The other key function of your abstract is to enable future researchers to identify whether your research is going to be relevant to their topic.

Here are the criteria I use to evaluate an abstract.

- What do you understand the research topic to be?
- What was the research question?
- What discipline(s) or field(s) is the dissertation located within?
- Given the title of the dissertation, what areas of literature would you have expected it to consult?
- What methodology and methods were used to carry out the research?
- How good a match do you think there is between the research question and methods?
- What are the main findings?
- What conclusions has the dissertation reached?

It is unlikely you will get the abstract right first time. It can be helpful to use these criteria to critique abstracts in dissertations you have read. Ask a fellow student to critique your abstract. Ensure your supervisor is totally happy.

The final check for consistency

The most difficult thing to deal with as an examiner is when the purpose of the dissertation seems to evolve as the argument unfolds. Do you mark against the title and abstract or do you judge the dissertation against one of the other definitions of the research question that emerge?

The most important check is to ensure that you are totally consistent about what you say about the purpose of the research at each of the following key points:

- Title.
- Abstract.
- Introductory chapter.
- Initial statement of research question.
- Methodology chapter.
- Answer to research question.
- Concluding chapter.

What examiners look for

In this section, I will attempt the difficult task of arousing your sympathy towards your examiners. They are the first and most important audience for your dissertation and this chapter has already suggested some ways in which you can make it easier for them to view your work positively. For a doctorate you will have two examiners: an internal from your university and an external from another university. Masters dissertations are usually only marked internally.

Reading from the back

As I open the bubble-wrap envelope in which the dissertation arrives, I always start by opening the back page and skim-reading the bibliography. I will confess to the egotism of wanting to know if I get a mention. After all, if the supervisor thinks I'm the right person to examine this, then surely I deserve a mention. At a more worthy level the bibliography tells me how much overlap there is between what this student is presenting and what I already know. I'm hoping for a reasonable overlap that means we are likely to be on the same page, but I'm also hoping to learn something new, and so I'm pleased when I see an area of literature with which I'm unfamiliar.

Next I want to know whether this is going to be straight-forward or problematic to examine, so I skim-read the conclusions.[2] If I'm left with a feeling of confidence, I look forward to the time I have set aside in my diary to do the examining. If I am left feeling uneasy, I book some extra time into my diary as my examiner's report is going to take some careful drafting.

Setting expectations

As already indicated, when the time comes to read the dissertation I start by noting what my expectations are having read the title and abstract. I also look at the criteria for the award of the degree, which will have been included in the envelope. They vary slightly between universities, so I need to be sure I am focusing on what this university feels is important. I have a separate piece of paper ready to list corrections.

The next thing I want to do is get an overview of the argument. I spend some time studying the contents page, so I am familiar with the structure. In a doctorate I would then turn to the introduction and conclusions, where I would expect to see the argument summarized. In a Masters dissertation I would read the introduction but also look at the top and tail of each chapter to see how the argument builds.

Having equipped myself with an understanding of the student's intentions, I make my first cup of coffee.

Making notes against the examining criteria and expectations

This part of the process is the one I save up for train journeys if I can. I read each chapter in turn and make notes about how

---

2 Some doctoral students have a section in their conclusions that critically evaluates their research against the criteria for the degree. This makes me unreasonably happy.

my expectations are being met and whether the chapter contains any evidence, positive or negative, relating to the examining criteria. My ideal is to complete this part of the process at no more than two sittings, but sometimes real life intervenes, and I'm grateful when the dissertation is well structured, so I can pick up where I left off.

Examiners' reports and vivas

When I am back at my desk, I review my notes and decide what comments I will make in my written examiner's report on the examining criteria. If there is to be a viva, I also make a list of questions I would like to ask the student. If I have any doubts that the student will pass, I take particular care to identify what I understand to be the main problems and how I will test the student's understanding of them in the viva. I also type up the list of corrections I have found – the longer that list is, the more tedious the task and the potential for me to lapse into irritation.

By now you should have a sense that this is a serious investment of time. Examiners are paid an honorarium, but it is not remuneration for the level of effort involved. Examiners also have to meet deadlines, which can mean reshuffling other priorities to have the examiner's report submitted on time.

If there is to be a viva, I am looking forward to meeting the real person behind the text and seeing how they deal with the issues I have identified. In the past, the examiner could also look forward to a slap up lunch before or after the viva, but now sadly most universities provide nothing more than standard buffet fare, and some even expect the supervisor to take you out for a modest pub lunch.[3] Trafford and Lesham (2008) contains valuable advice on preparing for a viva, and so here I

---

3 The University of Chester is an honourable exception. Needless to say my views as an examiner are not swayed.

will merely confirm that you do need to prepare. Don't allow your brain to go on holiday between submission and viva.

After the viva

Only about eight per cent of doctoral candidates emerge from a viva without further work to do (Trafford and Lesham 2008). The viva is an important milestone deserving of maximum support, but it is likely that afterwards there will be a period of three months to one year when you are doing further work. You are usually given three months for minor corrections, which involve putting right any typos and tightening up your argument or conclusions with a paragraph here and there. Major corrections are usually given a year and involve significant rewriting of part of what you have done. This will require intensive work with your supervisor to identify what needs to be done and an action plan for doing it. Minor corrections will be signed off by the internal examiner. Major corrections will need the approval of both examiners and possibly a second viva. Rarely candidates will be asked to revise and submit their whole dissertation in order to be considered for the degree. As in the whole process, your response to feedback at this point is vital. As an examiner you are keenly aware of the effort the student has invested and so you want them to 'come up with the goods'. I am always happy to clarify an examiner's report to help the student over that final line.

Disseminating your research

The sense of relief when you know you have passed is intense and it can be tempting to draw a line immediately. However, you have decided to research practice because you wanted to bring about change, and so it is important that before you take that well-earned break, you draw up the plan for disseminating your research, ideally with input from your supervisor and mentor.

The key question to ask yourself is: 'Who do I most want to communicate with and what are they likely to read?'

Ensuring an impact on practice

It can be tempting to think that you can give your dissertation to people to read. A dissertation is a technical document designed to prove your competence as a researcher. It takes a long time to get to the questions that fellow practitioners will want answering, namely: What did you find out and what should we do about it? It is therefore usually quicker in the end to write a separate report designed to answer those two questions. It can have appendices summarizing the reading you did and outlining your methodology and methods.

An effective way of disseminating to practitioners can be through learning events where they can try out new approaches or discuss their practice in relation to a model you have proposed.

Seeking an impact on policy

It is common for practitioners to identify that changes to the policies that affect their area of practice are needed if practice is to move on. Your research may well have identified who the policy makers are you need to influence and what changes you are seeking. Again, it is unlikely that they will read a whole dissertation, and so you need to design a document that will influence them and is specific in its requests for change.

This sort of report needs an executive summary that summarizes the recommendations being made in no more than one side. You also need tactics as to how you will get the report read and discussed by the right people.

Publication

Practical theology and the study of ministry and mission are still developing fields and so you are highly likely to have produced something original. This means it is important to get your work published so that others can learn from it and build upon it. You should brainstorm with your supervisor and mentor the possible outlets for what you have to say and then select a manageable number. These are likely to include: academic journals, practitioner journals and newsletters, books, conference papers leading to book chapters, web-based publication in blogs or on websites. It can take some time to get published so start while your data is fresh.

Each outlet for publication will have its own audience and guidelines that are there to help you target that audience with what you write. Here your skills in editing your own work come into their own, as you will have to take the dissertation into which you put so much love and care apart and identify which bits can be rewritten for which purpose.

Don't stop me now

After about a year you will start to consolidate the benefits of your research for your own practice and intellectual development. You should find yourself reading more widely, being critical of research presented to you as 'the answer', encouraging colleagues in their own learning and development and seeking new opportunities to develop your own practice and that of others. This consolidation often leads to some people realizing that their heart is in their practice and they wish to continue to develop it in the same or different contexts, or for others that they wish to move into a role where they either manage or develop the practice of others. This greater certainty about the contribution you can make to ministry and mission is one of the great benefits of learning to research.

Decisions following this chapter

- What have I already learned about myself as a writer and how can I make use of that reflection in writing up my research?

- How can I work most effectively with my supervisor at this stage?

- How do I best work out what I think about something – talking or writing?

- How can I improve my editing skills?

- Is my abstract as good as I can make it?

- Have I checked the coherence of the whole dissertation?

- Have I got the necessary academic and emotional support in place for the run-up to and aftermath of the viva?

- What are my plans for disseminating my research?

10

Documentary Analysis

To transform heart-felt inner experience into a theological resource the method employs journal-writing, personal letters, verbatim accounts of pastoral encounters, spiritual autobiography and other contemporary forms of creative writing, as the means to 'turn-life-into-text'. Such texts can be described as 'living human documents' in the sense that they are authentic accounts of lived experience presented in a form that can be read and analysed. They do not only contain the perspectives of their authors but also witness to their conversational encounters with other people, other world-views and with God . . . (Graham et al. 2005, describing one form of documentary analysis in *Theological Reflection: Methods*, p. 18)

This final chapter on methods looks at documentary analysis in church-based research. It gives an overview of the method and ends with a bibliography of suggested further reading.

Introduction to documentary analysis

Documents are all around us. They are an integral part of our daily lives and concerns. 'People keep diaries, send letters, make quilts, take photos, dash off memos, compose auto/biographies, construct web sites, scrawl graffiti, publish their memoirs, write letters, compose CVs, leave suicide notes, film and video diaries, inscribe memorials on tombstones, shoot films, paint pictures, make tapes and try to record their personal dreams . . .' (Plummer 2001, in McCulloch 2004, p. 1). Documentary analysis is a method of extracting data from written and visual sources for the purposes of research. These sources can be official documents of the state or Church or personal documents giving unique insight into people's human stories, historical narratives, cultural ideologies and encounters with the divine. Some documents are produced specifically for research purposes, like the opening quotation suggests; other documents are already in existence and are either public or private material which the researcher uses, once permission is sought. There are many different types of data each with their own possibilities and limitations for researchers: primary, secondary, solicited, unsolicited, paper-based, virtual, archival records, books, periodicals, works of fiction, official data and proceedings, reports and diaries (see McCulloch 2004).

Annotated checklist for using documentary analysis

Below is a checklist for using documents in church-based research.

Case study 1

Analysing documents in the context of ministry and mission

People who use written documents in their research need to be critically reflective practitioners who are attentive to the ways in which their reading of a document is shaped by their world view and theological standpoint. People bring all sorts of assumptions and perspectives to the task of reading documentation. Likewise, authors of documents can reveal much about their own perspectives and standpoints. It is likely that you are more equipped than you think for the task of using documentary analysis. Many theological sub-disciplines, for example, have their conventions and strategies for reading text which you may be familiar with: looking at the author and the world behind the text, looking at the text

---

itself and the world of the text, and finally looking at the world in front of the text and how the reader responds to it (see John Barton's interpretative map, 1984). As with the different styles of interviews, a spectrum exists in relation to the extent to which data collected is factual or descriptive.

Locate your documents

There are important issues to think through before using documents in research:

- Be clear about the author, their status, their sponsorship and underlying motivations.
- Be clear about the authenticity of the text, the date of the document/website and when it was last updated.
- Be clear about how genuine and credible the documents are. Is the evidence clear and comprehensive?
- Be clear about how representative the document is and of whom?
- Has it been edited and if so by whom and when?
- Establish how sensitive and accessible the information is – is it in the public domain? Does it raise copyright or data-protection issues?

The relevance of these questions will vary depending upon the document being assessed.

Types of documents

Types of documents in church-based research might include:

Grey literature

Faith communities and church-based organizations produce huge quantities of grey literature such as newsletters, mission action plans, annual reports and policy documents. These documents can be researched in their own right or they can provide a useful starting point in research outlining the espoused theology of an organization, which can then be compared to data from other methods such as interviews that record the operant theology (Cameron et al. 2010). It is worth remembering that grey literature gets out of date quickly.

Liturgical texts

Liturgical texts can reveal a huge amount about the espoused and normative theologies of an organization or church. Different denominations have different levels of formality and authority attached to their liturgical texts. Once again, there are three ways to read into liturgical documents – looking at the author, looking at the text itself and looking at how people receive the text (See Case study 2 in Chapter 4, which focuses on liturgy).

Reflective writing

All sorts of documents can be used for theological reflection, as outlined in Graham et al. (2005). Personal journals, Christian autobiographical writing, verbatim methods, and other constructive narrative approaches are all good examples of data. Questions of confidentiality need careful consideration.

Case study 2

Locating operant theology through people's reflective writing

London Jesuit Volunteers is a small volunteer agency based at a Jesuit Centre in Mayfair placing people in voluntary social-justice placements and offering a monthly peer-group support meeting for theological reflection rooted within the

Ignatian tradition. In research looking at the values under-pinning this approach, nine volunteers were asked to write a side of A4 about a significant experience or encounter they had had in their placements (with all names removed to pre-serve anonymity). These were then circulated to an insider and an outsider team for theological reflection. The docu-ments provided an astonishingly rich and intimate collec-tion of personal reflections on faith-in-action. They helped the organization see that their espoused theology was closely aligned to the operant theology of these volunteers as dis-closed in these texts.

Websites

Websites are key 'texts' for finding out more about what an organization does and what it stands for, but they must be used with caution. Church websites vary in terms of how regularly they are updated. This can lead to distorted perceptions about the vibrancy of a faith community without a follow-up visit or interview. For example, investment in online resources might be an indication of a community's *ad extra* commitments to mission or simply a reflection of the availability of financial resources or an individual enthusiasm.

Over the past decade there has been an explosion in virtual documents and online discussion forums. These documents can be read in two ways – for facts and for the subtle social, polit-ical and cultural differentiations they reveal.

Criticism of documentary analysis

The limitation of documentary analysis is that documents can only ever tell part of a story. They are static text. They don't necessarily reflect 'actual practice' or the operant theology of either the author or the reader. Documents use words that have multiple meanings or interpretations depending upon the reader.

It is necessary to confirm the credibility of a source – including their sponsorship and accuracy. Finally, analysing documents as data can be a challenge with coding reflecting the different perspectives of author, readers and researcher. Documents are best used in the context of a multi-method approach. They can be cheap, readily accessible data to underpin your research.

Bibliography

Generic chapters in books

Bryman, A. (2012), *Social Research Methods*, 4th edn, Oxford: Oxford University Press, ch. 23.
This chapter introduces the use of documents in research ranging from personal, official and virtual documents. It looks at how to evaluate text, through qualitative content analysis, semiotics and hermeneutics. Chapter 28 also looks at e-research and the implications of using the internet to collect data.

Denscombe, M. (2010), *The Good Research Guide for Small-scale Social Research Projects*, 4th edn, Maidenhead: Open University Press, Part II, ch. 12.
A useful chapter looking at accessibility, credibility and validity of documents in research, including image-based research.

Specialist books and articles

McCulloch, G. (2004), *Documentary Research: In Education, History and the Social Sciences*, London: Routledge Falmer.
This small, dense book argues for the importance of documentary research in the fields of education, history and social sciences. Chapters explore among other things: a historical review of the method; ethical issues; use of records and archives; printed media and literature; diaries, letters and autobiographies. It concludes with a recommendation for documentary analysis to be part of a multi-method approach.

The use of documentary analysis in practical theology

Graham, E., Walton, H. et al. (2005), *Theological Reflection: Methods*, London: SCM Press.
This is an excellent exposition of the use of documents in different forms of theological method – such as personal living human documents, canonical texts, public theology and the correlational method, corporate theological reflection and theology in the vernacular.

Receptive Ecumenism and the Local Church: A Regional Comparative Research Project (Centre for Catholic Studies, Durham University), www.dur.ac.uk/theology.religion/ccs/projects/receptiveecumenism/ .
This major empirical project in the North of England used a multi-method approach to exploring receptive ecumenism. The first phase gathered key documentation from participating denominations. The later stages moved on to detailed ethnographic case-studies of two congregations from each of the denominations.

Ahmed, S., Banks, S. and Duce, C. (2007), 'Walking Alongside Young People: Challenges and Opportunities for Faith Communities, A Research Report on North East England', Durham, www.dur.ac.uk/resources/sass/Walking%20Along side%20Young%20People.pdf.
This two-year empirical project in the North East of England (Community and Youth Work, Durham University) looked at faith-based youth work. It began with a large region-wide scoping exercise of gathering documentary data. It involved collecting leaflets, checking websites, gathering published grey literature on youth work across faith communities so as to set the scene for participatory action research. The quality and nature of these sources varied considerably.

Conclusion

This conclusion outlines steps that you can take to consolidate what you have read in this book. We suggest creating a timetable for your research, setting up expectations with your nearest and dearest about the implications of your research and finally ensuring that you embark upon the process with the right support mechanisms in place.

Turning the six-point plan into a timetable

Revisit the six-point plan on pages 4–6 and work out how the stages will fit into the reality of your life. A good place to start is to identify the fixed points that you cannot change. These may include the final submission date, the opportunity to do fieldwork, the chance of time away from work. The next stage is to look at your day job and voluntary and domestic responsibilities to see where the peaks and troughs are likely to be during your research period. For those in ministry, Christmas and Easter often bring additional work and so it may be difficult to sustain research during those periods. Look at the time that is left and decide whether each stage can be undertaken satisfactorily in the time available. Build in contingency time, in case things don't go as planned.

If this planning exercise reveals that what you hope to do does not match the time available to do it, you have two possible courses of action. One is to negotiate a reduction in your existing responsibilities to free up time. The other is to reduce the size and ambition of the research project while checking with your supervisor that you would still meet the expectations of the degree programme.

Setting realistic expectations with family, friends, colleagues and research stakeholders

A research project can feel like a long motorway journey with your back-seat drivers constantly asking: Are we nearly there yet? It is not uncommon for people in practical theology to be the first person in their immediate family to study at post-graduate level or to be working in a setting where knowledge of research is limited. It can be helpful to make those around you aware of the main junctions you will pass on the journey and that it really isn't completely over until the graduation ceremony has happened. The following are some useful milestones to mark along the way:

- End of the literature review.
- End of the data collection.
- Deciding what you think of it all.
- Completed first draft.
- Submission and examination.
- Resubmission.
- Letter confirming examiners' verdict.
- Graduation ceremony.

Finally you need to prepare people for the fact that you will be disseminating your research, and so further patience is needed, while you ensure your research has the desired impact.

Finding the support you need to enjoy your research project

This book has referred regularly to your relationship with your supervisor. That is clearly a vital relationship in the research process. However, it is worth thinking about other forms of support you will need.

If you are working as well as researching, you will need someone in your workplace who you can negotiate with about the additional pressures that the research will place upon you. Ideally that will be a sympathetic line manager or the chair of any committee that you report to. However, sadly there are many ministers who work in settings where the empathy of that person cannot be relied upon. It may be necessary to find a colleague or perhaps someone recently retired who can listen with genuine interest to the work dilemmas which your research creates. It is impossible at the outset to be fully aware of all the implications, so you need someone to whom you can return as the situation develops for further encouragement and support. If you are in a role with limited supervision, you may need someone to help you be firm with yourself and say no to things which while desirable cannot be accommodated alongside the extra work generated by the research.

It is also worth recruiting some general human sympathy about the research process. It would be natural to turn to family and friends for this, but if they are unaware of the pressures that research creates, it would be good to find someone who has already done a research project who can act as a mentor. The mentor's role is to listen to the unfolding of each step in the process and encourage you to develop helpful tactics. They can celebrate with you as you reach each milestone and commiserate when something does not work as well as expected. They can listen to you as you share your thinking and make supportive noises so you develop your train of thought.

A research project is a lot of self-imposed hard work. Much of what is needed to succeed is hard work, persistence and attention to detail rather than intellectual genius. Try to secure the funding you need before you start, as another way of relieving pressure. Keep in view your hopes about how practice will be developed as a result of your work.

Finally you will need your support network to help you return to the 'new normal'. The intensity of the research project has gone, but some of your habits, practices and attitudes will have changed, and you need scope to build upon the development that has taken place.

Parting of the way: reflections from the companions

We have enjoyed designing, writing and editing this book together. It builds upon three years of working as colleagues in which we both developed as researchers and writers. We hope you have gained something from our companionship throughout this book. We have tried to be honest about the joys and challenges of research, but give sufficient encouragement to develop your own practice as a researcher.

Helen Cameron

I come to the end of writing this book with a certain amount of sadness. I've enjoyed teaching research methods in the classroom and particularly the intensive courses Catherine and I taught together. It is sad to leave behind something which has been so enriching. As a talker, I've developed a lot of my own thinking about research in dialogue with those I've taught, and so I want to express my appreciation to them.

I also come to the end with a feeling of excitement. Practical theology and the study of ministry and mission are at a stage where a much wider range of approaches are developing and the breadth of what is being studied is increasing. I hope people will disagree with what we have written or see things differently and that that will feed into the debate about the relationship between theology and practice.

Reflecting on the book, I feel that the chapters I have written have been more directive than I intended. I think this is because I have met more students who have suffered from supervision that didn't deal with difficulties than those receiving over-critical supervision.

I have returned to the world of practice firmly committed to research, both my own and that of others. I can see the huge potential of research to inform my own practice and how so often a little bit of research can go a long way in bringing about change.

Catherine Duce

It is satisfying to reach the end of a piece of research in practical theology and to discover that new insights have triggered fresh conversation and renewed curiosity about practice within a church community. I come to the end of this book with a fresher appreciation of the value of researching practice. It has been an enjoyable task to reflect upon my life experiences as a researcher.

Anyone who spends time doing a job that they love can develop a subconscious competence (and incompetence!) at the roles that they fulfil and the processes that they follow. It has been a helpful discipline to record my own practice and to think through why I do what I do. That said, I am painfully aware at times that the annotated checklists and the real-life case studies have seemed to contradict one another. 'Do as I say and not as I do!' is what I have wanted to write. My hope, however, is that this was less of a distraction and more of an encouragement not to shy away from the messiness of real-life research, rather to embrace it with integrity and with humour.

The wider church has much to learn from practical theology in this regard. Practical theology has a brave willingness to engage fearlessly with reality. Now that I am in full-time ministerial training I aspire to play my part in this engagement, first by becoming a curious curate.

Further Reading

It is impossible to do full justice to the range of research methods and techniques in a book of this length. We have urged you to look at the relevant shelves in the library and ask librarians for advice. However, this section contains a few additional titles that those we have taught have found useful.

Use of descriptive statistics

Blastland, M. and Dilnot, A. (2007), *The Tiger that Isn't: Seeing through a World of Numbers*, London: Profile Books.
British Religion in Numbers: see www.brin.ac.uk.
A useful portal for statistics on religion with guidelines on how various sources can be interpreted.

Case studies

Thomas, G. (2010), *How to do your Case Study: A Guide for Students and Researcher*, London: Sage.
Yin, R. K. (2008), *Case Study Research: Design and Methods*, London: Sage.

Evaluation

Kara, H. (2012), *Research and Evaluation for Busy Practitioners: A Time-saving Guide*, Bristol: Policy Press.

Researching vulnerable people

Etherington, K. (2004), *Becoming a Reflexive Researcher: Using Our Selves in Research*, London and Philadelphia, PA: Jessica Kingsley Publishers.

Holloway, W. and Jefferson, T. (2013), *Doing Qualitative Research Differently: A Psychosocial Approach*, 2nd edn, London: Sage.

Liamputtong, P. (2006), *Researching the Vulnerable: A Guide to Sensitive Research Methods*, London: Sage.

Writing up

Dunleavy, P. (2003), *Authoring a PhD: How to Plan, Draft, Write and Finish a Doctoral Thesis or Dissertation*, London: Palgrave Macmillan.

Fairbairn, G. and Winch, C. (2011), *Reading, Writing and Reasoning: A Guide for Students*, 3rd edn, Maidenhead: Open University Press.

Theological reflection

Bevans, S. (2002), *Models of Contextual Theology*, Maryknoll, NY: Orbis Books.

Killen, P. O. C. and de Beer, J. (2006), *The Art of Theological Reflection*, New York: Crossroad.

Thompson, J. with Pattison, S. et al. (2008), *SCM Studyguide to Theological Reflection*, London: SCM Press.

Appendix

Points for Practitioner Researchers Not Undertaking a Degree

Doing research outside a degree programme carries distinctive challenges, some of which we highlight here.

Ethics

What status is given to the people who take part in the research? If they are congregants, clients or colleagues, do they benefit from the research in any way? Are they represented in the writing up of the research in a way in which they would recognize as accurate, even if they would not accept your analysis?

Planning

Is the research planned in a way that includes those who will be affected by its results? If the aim is to develop practice, are the relevant practitioners given an opportunity to comment on the methodology and method? Is the interpretation of the data discussed in a way that the implications can be owned by practitioners?

Governance

Is the research properly authorized by the organization? Do those at a senior level accept the level of influence they will have over the outcomes of the research? Are they willing to see changes in practice happen as a result of the research? Is there agreement to address any ethically challenging issues that arise unexpectedly during the course of the research?

Research access

Have all the necessary stakeholders been consulted and where appropriate given consent to your access to the research setting? What do any obstacles tell you about the nature of the setting in which the practice is taking place?

Reporting

Will one research report be sufficient or do different stakeholders need different types of feedback on the research? Will the report end with the analysis of the data or proceed to recommendations? Whose role is it to receive and act upon the recommendations?

Impact

If the intention has been that the research would change practice, who is responsible for putting in place the relationships, policies, training, structures and other processes necessary for this to happen?

Support

Can you identify a 'critical friend' from outside the research setting, who can offer feedback and support?

Theological reflection

Ensure you use an approach appropriate to the setting that neither baffles nor patronizes participants.

Bibliography

Ahmed, S., Banks, S. and Duce, C. (2007), 'Walking Along-side Young People: Challenges and Opportunities for Faith Communities: A Research Report on North East England', Durham, www.dur.ac.uk/resources/sass/Walking%20Along side%20Young%20People.pdf.

Atherton, J. and Baker, C. et al. (2011), *Christianity and the New Social Order*, London: SPCK.

Barton, J. (1984), 'Classifying Biblical Criticism', *Journal for the Study of the Old Testament* 9(29), pp. 19–35.

Bennett, Z. (2004), *Incorrigible Plurality: Teaching Pastoral Theology in an Ecumenical Context*, Edinburgh: Contact Pastoral Trust.

Brown, C. G. (2009), *The Death of Christian Britain: Under-standing Secularisation 1800–2000*, London: Routledge.

Browning, D. S. (1991), *Fundamental Practical Theology: Descriptive and Strategic Proposals*, Minneapolis, MN: Fortress Press.

Bryman, A. (2012), *Social Research Methods*, 4th edn, Oxford: Oxford University Press.

Cameron, H. and Richter, P. et al. (eds) (2005), *Studying Local Churches: A Handbook*, London: SCM Press.

Cameron, H. and Bhatti, D. et al. (2010), *Talking about God in Practice: Theological Action Research and Practical Theology*, London: SCM Press.

Cameron, H. (2012), '"Life in all its Fullness" Engagement and Critique: Good News for Society', *Practical Theology* 5(1), pp. 11–26.

Cameron, H. and Reader, J. et al. (2012), *Theological Reflection for Human Flourishing: Public Theology and Pastoral Practice*, London: SCM Press.

Cameron, H. (2004), 'Are Congregations Associations? The Contribution of Organizational Studies to Congregational Studies', in Guest, M., Tusting, K., and Woodhead, L., (eds), *Congregational Studies in the UK: Christianity in a Post-Christian Context*, Aldershot: Ashgate, pp. 139–51.

Caperon, J. (2012), 'The Nature of the Ministry of School Chaplains in Church of England Secondary Schools', unpublished DProf thesis, Anglia Ruskin University.

Cartledge, M. J. (2010), *Testimony in the Spirit: Rescripting Ordinary Pentecostal Theology*, Farnham: Ashgate.

Creswell, J. W. (2003), *Research Design: Qualitative, Quantitative, and Mixed Methods Approaches*, London: Sage Publications.

Creswell, J. W. (2007), *Qualitative Inquiry and Research Design: Choosing Among Five Approaches*, London: Sage Publications.

Dahlberg, L. and McCraig, C. (2010), *Practical Research and Evaluation: A Start-to-Finish Guide for Practitioners*, London: Sage Publications.

Denscombe, M. (2010), *The Good Research Guide for Small-scale Social Research Projects*, 4th edn, Maidenhead: Open University Press.

Downey, M. (1997), *Understanding Christian Spirituality*, Mahwah, NJ: Paulist Press.

Duce, C. (2013), 'Church-based Work with the Homeless: A Theological Exploration of the Practices of Hospitality', *Practical Theology* 6(1), pp. 87–103.

EThOS – Electronic Theses Online Service at http://EThOs.bl.uk.

Forrester, D. (2005), *Theological Fragments: Explorations in Unsystematic Theology*, Edinburgh: T&T Clark.

Fulkerson, M. M. (2007), *Places of Redemption: Theology for a Worldly Church*, Oxford. Oxford University Press.

Goodhew, D. (2012), *Church Growth in Britain*, Farnham: Ashgate.

Graham, E. L. (2002), *Transforming Practice: Pastoral Theology in an Age of Uncertainty*, Eugene, OR: Wipf and Stock.

Graham, E. L. and Walton, H. et al. (2005), *Theological Reflection: Methods*, London: SCM Press.

Graham, E. L. and Walton, H. et al. (2007), *Theological Reflection: Sources*, London: SCM Press.

Guest, M. (2007), *Evangelical Identity and Contemporary Culture: A Congregational Study in Innovation*, Carlisle: Paternoster Press.

Hart, C. (1998), *Doing a Literature Review: Releasing the Social Science Research Imagination*, London: Sage Publications.

Jackson, B. (2005), *The Road to Growth: Towards a Thriving Church*, London: Church House Publishing.

Knott, K. (2005), 'Insider/Outsider Perspectives', in Hinnells, J. (ed.), *The Routledge Companion to the Study of Religion*, Abingdon: Routledge.

Krueger, R. and Casey, M. A. (2009), *Focus Groups: A Practical Guide for Applied Research*, 4th edn, Thousand Oaks, CA: Sage Publications.

Lindbeck, G. A. (2009), *The Nature of Doctrine: Religion and Theology in a Postliberal Age*, Louisville, KY: Westminster/John Knox Press.

May, T. (2001), *Social Research: Issues, Methods and Process*, Maidenhead: Open University Press.

Mellot, D. M. (2009), *I Was and I Am Dust: Penitente Practices as a Way of Knowing*, Collegeville, MN: Liturgical Press.

Moschella, M. C. (2008), *Ethnography as a Pastoral Practice: An Introduction*, Cleveland, OH: The Pilgrim Press.

Moschella, M. C. (2012), 'Ethnography', in Miller-McLemore, B. (ed.), *The Wiley-Blackwell Companion to Practical Theology*, Chichester: Wiley-Blackwell.

Pallant, D. (2012), *Keeping Faith in Faith-Based Organisations: A Practical Theology of Salvation Army Health Ministry*, Eugene OR: Wipf and Stock.

Pattison, S. (2000), 'Some Straw for the Bricks: A Basic Introduction to Theological Reflection', in Woodward, J. and

Pattison, S. (eds), *The Blackwell Reader in Pastoral and Practical Theology*, Oxford: Blackwell, pp. 135–45.

Phillips, E. and Pugh, D. S. (2010), *How to get a PhD: A Handbook for Students and their Supervisors*, Milton Keynes: Open University Press.

Plummer, K. (2001), *Documents of Life 2: An Invitation to a Critical Humanism*, London: Sage.

Ridley, D. (2008), *The Literature Review: A Step-by-step Guide for Students*, London: Sage Publications.

Robinson, T. (2009), 'Liturgy and Identity: What does the Liturgy Make of Me? Interpreting the Effect of the Liturgy on Personal Identity in a Fresh Expression', Unpublished MA in Ministry, Oxford Brookes University.

Rodd, S. (2011), '"With one accord?" – A Case Study in Twenty-first Century Rural Ecumenism: An Exploration of Existing and Possible Ecumenical Collaboration in a Wiltshire Village, as Perceived by the Community', unpublished MA in Ministry, Oxford Brookes University.

Saldona, J. (2009), *The Coding Manual for Qualitative Researchers*, London: Sage Publications.

Scharen, C. and Vigen, A. M. (2011), *Ethnography as Christian Theology and Ethics*, London: Continuum.

Smith, N.-J. (2008), *Achieving your Professional Doctorate*, Maidenhead: Open University Press.

Stoddart, E. (2005), 'What is Our Liturgy Doing to Us? The After Effects of Worship', *Studia Liturgica* vol. 35, pp. 100–10.

Swinton, J. and Mowat, H. (2006), *Practical Theology and Qualitative Research*, London: SCM Press.

Trafford, V. and Leshem, S. (2008), *Stepping Stones to Achieving your Doctorate*, Maidenhead: Open University Press.

van der Ven, J. (1990), *Practical Theology: An Empirical Approach*, Leuven: Peeters Press.

Village, A. (2007), *The Bible and Lay People: An Empirical Approach to Ordinary Hermeneutics*, Aldershot: Ashgate Publishing.

Ward, F. (2004), 'The Messiness of Studying Congregations using Ethnographic Methods', in Guest, M., Tusting, K. and

Woodhead, L. (eds), *Congregational Studies in the UK: Christianity in a Post-Christian Context*, Aldershot: Ashgate, pp. 125–38

Ward, P. (2008), *Participation and Mediation: A Practical Theology for the Liquid Church*, London: SCM Press.

Ward, P. (ed.) (2012), *Perspectives on Ecclesiology and Ethnography*, Grand Rapids, MI: Eerdmans.

Watkins, C. and Shepherd, B. (2013), 'The Challenge of "Fresh Expressions" to Ecclesiology: Reflections from the Practice of Messy Church', *Ecclesial Practices: The Journal of Ecclesiology and Ethnography* 1(1), pp. 92–110.

Author Index

Subject Index

Reflexivity xvii, xxx, 90–1, 118, 130

Research design 3, 33–5, 37, 46, 81, 97, 106

Research journal xxvi–xxvii, xxxi, 15, 33, 35, 47

Research proposals 28, 35–7, 41, 43, 46, 49, 121

Research question 2–5, 8, 17, 24, 28–9, 31, 33, 35, 37, 45, 47–9, 51–3, 75, 79, 81, 82, 85, 95, 98, 105, 107–8, 116, 121, 125, 129–30, 132–3

Research saturation 60

Research timetable 5, 15, 36, 39, 80, 90, 111, 147

Researcher xiv–xviii, xxiv, 4, 17, 21, 33, 39, 47, 50–1, 54, 56–9, 62, 84, 100, 125, 130, 137, 150, 154

Sabbatical researchers xvi, xix, 6, 154–5

Sampling 18–20, 85, 98–9, 111, 118

Scripture xiii, 13, 45, 77

Six-point plan 4–6, 10, 147–8

Social Science xx, xxviii, 12, 44, 145

Student xv– xvi, xvii, xxii, xxiv, 7, 10–1, 36–7, 40–3, 45, 47, 51–

2, 65, 67, 76, 82, 108, 122–4, 132–6

Supervision 6, 52, 121–2, 149–50

Supervisors xv–xvi, xxv, xxviii, 4, 6, 10–11, 36–7, 40–4, 49, 65, 70–1, 79–80, 85, 105–7, 121–4, 132, 136–9, 148

Support xv, xvii, xxiii, 36, 38, 42, 48, 122, 136, 139, 148–50, 155

Telephone interviews 85–6

Theological reflection xxviii–xxxi, 13, 46–7, 83, 106, 143–4, 153, 155

Theology in Four Voices see Four Voices

Tradition xxii, xxvii–xxx, 12, 32–3, 45–7, 49, 77, 106,

Transcription 91, 102

Transferable skills xxiv–xxvi, xxxi, 111

Triangulation 34

Value xxvii, 12, 32, 75, 82, 91, 109

World views ix, 13, 28–30, 91, 140

Writing xvii, xxv, 6, 9, 48, 74, 78–80, 104–5, 121–139, 143, 153